" Carmeca
Be Blessed!
Mary A.

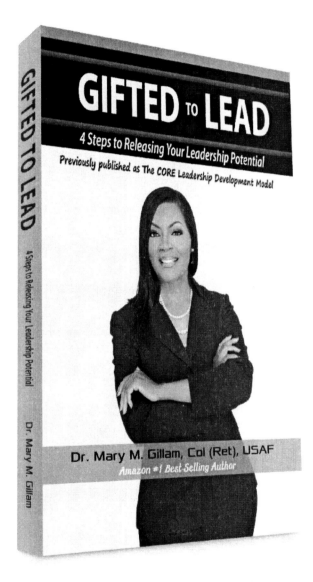

&

"We have all been endowed with gifts and talents. Yet, it is up to us to develop those gifts and release those talents."

—*Dr. Mary Gillam*

Passion, Opportunity, Faith

#1 Amazon Bestselling Author

Gifted to Lead

4 *Steps to Releasing Your Leadership Potential*

Dr. Mary M. Gillam, Col (Ret), USAF

For additional books by the Author and booking information:

- Website: http://www.m2gleadershipbiz.com
- Email: DrMaryGillam@m2gleadershipbiz.com
- Email: gillammm@verizon.net
- Author's Amazon Book Page information
  www.amazon.com/author/marygillam

- Author's Electronic Press Kit information
  http://epresskitz.com/DrMaryMGillam

Books are available on Amazon, Kindle, Barnes & Noble, Create Space Publishing and other book distribution sites.

Author Photo by: Jackie Hicks, Fond Memories Photography

Printed in the United States of America

ॐ

"The art of genuine leadership is developing the next generation of leaders."

—*Dr. Mary Gillam*

ॐ

Other Books by Dr. Mary M. Gillam

- ✓ The Development Model
- ✓ 14 Jewels of Dynamic Leadership
- ✓ Information Warfare: Combating the Threat in the 21st Century
- ✓ Exploring the Impact of the Clinger-Cohen Act of 1996 on Information Technology Governance (Dissertation)
- ✓ Self-Publishing: Lessons Learned From My Journey
- ✓ 31 Gems of Poetic Inspiration
- ✓ I Never Said Good-bye
- ✓ A Jewel Collage of Poetry
- ✓ Women Stop the Chase: Let God's Man Find You Expanded Edition
- ✓ Women Stop the Chase: Let God's Man Find You
- ✓ Women Stop the Chase: Let God's Man Find You Work Book

❧

"Passion, purpose, preparation, and perspiration can help you win the leadership challenge."

—*Dr. Mary Gillam*

∂

DEDICATION

To the one who gave me the vision and wisdom to help inspire and motivate emerging leaders to embrace their gifts and talents and release their God given leadership potential.

પ

ACKNOWLEDGMENTS

T his book captures a lifetime of personal experiences and knowledge instilled in me by various leaders, mentors, teachers, peers, coaches, friends, family and most importantly God. It is through these lenses, that I developed a model that will help individuals to discover their gifts and hidden *leadership potential*. I believe that God places an enormous amount of potential inside all of us. However, what we do to cultivate that potential depends on us.

I am eternally grateful to everyone who invested their precious time to hear my idea, read and review my manuscript, and most of all— believed in my ability to produce this work. Without your recommendations and guidance along the way, I would have wavered in fulfilling my dream.

Finally, to everyone who chose to purchase this book, I want to extend my deepest gratitude. May the contents of the book be a blessing, and enrich your lives continuously. For you are destined for greatness. Only time will tell if you are the next history making leader just waiting to be discovered.

As an experienced and seasoned leader, and retired Air Force Colonel, I cannot help but salute each of you.

৵

"Recognize and embrace the leadership potential that is inside of you so that you can reach the destination that is before you."

—*Dr. Mary M. Gillam*

࿐

CONTENTS

❦

PREFACE

October 14, 2013 will impact my life forever. Earlier that morning, I received an email from a female military officer name Johnna. Although I was now retired from the Air Force, it was wonderful to hear from her. As I read the email, emotions began to swell up inside. What she wrote in her email literally validated everything that I have strived to do in leadership development over the course of 30⁺ years of working with people. To put things in perspective, in 1999, Johnna worked directly for me when I commanded a special duty organization in the Air Force. It was my second command tour.

Johnna was an exceptional young officer, extremely talented and full of leadership potential. As her immediate supervisor, I recognized that trait instantly within her. Over the years, I followed her outstanding military career. She would later reach the distinguished rank of Lieutenant Colonel.

Now that I have sparked your interest, you are probably wondering, "What was so powerful about this email?" Let me share with you an excerpt. Johnna wrote:

Colonel Gillam,

As I approach my official [military] retirement ceremony this weekend, I've been thinking about the folks that played important parts in my development—**YOU** are one of those people. I just wanted to take a moment to say **thank you**."

—*Johnna*

Can you imagine how I felt reading that email? At the time, Johnna worked for me, she was a new Captain. I had the honor of officiating over her promotion ceremony. Many years had transpired since we worked together. Yet, from her note, it was obvious that I had made a positive impact on her life and vice versa.

Over the course of my career, I have received numerous testimonials from people like Johnna. As a leader (who sincerely cares about people), there is nothing more exhilarating than to hear that you made a positive difference in another's life.

Prior to retiring from the Air Force, I received numerous gifts to include a book of memorabilia. As a leader, mentor, and friend, some of the notes were so touching that I wanted to include one of them. Although I was retiring, it was wonderful to hear that I had impacted the lives of so many people. I am who I am because of Christ who lives in me.

Colonel Gillam,

I have been blessed with good management for most of my 35 working years, but I think **you put the bar up higher than anyone.** You truly live the Wingman Concept. It is easy for management to say they're there to help or they have an open door – but you gave us your all…all the time. I cannot tell you what that meant to me. You are an amazing person.

Ma'am, I'm so glad we got to work together. As strange as it may seem, you allowed us to get to know you and think of you as a friend. That's something pretty amazing to find in a boss."

—Gail K.

As I continued to flip through the book, I was astounded at the number of comments that reflected the same degree of sentiment.

It had been several years since I read the book, so to be reminded of those special tributes was overwhelming.

Having spent many years working with people in various capacities, you learn how to lead, manage, inspire, encourage, and motivate individuals to grow and develop beyond their present state. As an effective leader, your goal is to be a positive role model and mentor.

Why did I share these stories? The answer is simple. As I contemplated writing another book on leadership, I wanted to first share with you a little about my own personal leadership journey. What better way to present that information, than to hear from those in whom I had the privilege to serve, and who could attest to my leadership and professional acumen.

Now, why did I write this book? What problem will the information presented in the book solve? As a seasoned and experienced leader in the military, government, and the private sector, I have worked in numerous organizations and discovered some leadership "heroes." These individuals were primed for a leadership role. They just needed someone to give them a chance to develop their leadership skills, but to recognize their potential.

With a combined 30+ years of information technology, leadership and management experience, I believe—no, I am convinced that there are many people with latent/undeveloped leadership potential. They possess an inherent degree of undiscovered leadership talent. Unfortunately, sometimes, the potential lies dormant and simply requires an external source to coach them through their leadership journey.

INTRODUCTION

D ifferent empirical studies have documented that over the next five to ten years about 50 percent of all government agency managers will be eligible for retirement. This number has circulated across the federal government for years leaving many leaders and managers to speculate on how to fill the leadership gap The government accountability office (GAO) highlighted this concern in numerous critical skills and competency assessment reports (GAO-13-188, January 17, 2013).

Given this pending shortfall in leadership talent, it is imperative that organizations continue to invest in programs that will promote leadership cultivation and development. These programs must be designed to generate a positive return on investment (ROI) for both the individual and the organization. Accountability for training outcomes is essential for organizational and personal growth.

Given the state of the economy today, organizations cannot afford to invest in training that produces no measurable return. In order to fill the pending leadership void, there has to be evidence documenting positive results from the leadership training. Therefore, implementing effective tools and techniques that can help individuals *grow as leaders* is a positive long-term investment in human capital leadership development.

As a leader with a passion for developing people, my goal for writing *Gifted to Lead: 4 Steps to Releasing Your Leadership Potential* was multifaceted. Initially, I wanted to share my personal journey and that of others as to how one can triumph against the odds and become a leader. Given my pedigree, who would have imagined that a little farm girl from North Carolina could lead anything. That is why innovation, diversity and inclusion in leadership development matters. There are hidden leaders all around us, and I want to help expose them and their talents.

Determined to help others discover their leadership abilities, I designed a four-step leadership development model called **CORE**, which I describe in this book. This simple-to-use and understand model will help individuals to transform their thinking and overcome their fear of leading. The model will inspire and empower men and women to cultivate their gifts and talents. Finally, the model will also challenge individuals to activate their passion and release their leadership potential.

How Can This Model Benefit You?

The CORE Leadership Development Model is a simple four-step process that enables individuals from across a broad spectrum of organizations, federal, state, and local governments, schools, churches, the military, and mentoring/intern programs to explore and develop their leadership potential. As you will discover in the book, the attributes of the model are presented at a level that can provide organizations with positive returns on their human capital investment. Since the concept is easy to understand, the model can be taught, and presented in different forums.

Figure 1 depicts the four components of the CORE Leadership Development Model. They are: Cause, Opportunity, Response, and Evaluation. Each step of the model or framework is described in subsequent chapters.

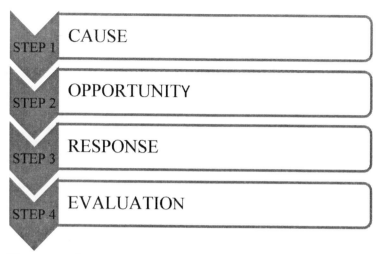

Figure 1: The CORE Leadership Development Model

Before proceeding further, let me describe the layout of the book. Part I discusses the Leadership Dilemma. Part II describes in-depth the CORE Leadership Development Model. Part III expounds on the importance of building a diverse leadership team via innovation, diversity, and inclusion. Finally, chapter 10 presents some general conclusions.

Now, let me ask you, "Are you ready to become the **"break-out"** leader that others will want to follow?" Let's find out together.

&

"Great Leaders value the importance of a good name."

—*Dr. Mary M. Gillam*

"A good name is rather to be chosen than great riches, and loving favor rather than silver and gold." (Proverbs 22:1, KJV)

ھ

PART I

The Leadership Dilemma

✓ Understanding Leadership?

✓ Uncommon Leaders: Triumph

Against the Odds

✓ Leadership Characteristics that

People Value

ॐ

CHAPTER 1

Understanding Leadership

When you think of a leader, what image or person comes to mind? Is it the President of the United States (POTUS), congressman, pastor, teacher, military member, corporate executive, principal, football coach, or is it the little elderly lady who has spent years mentoring girls from broken homes? Could the answer to this question be you?   If your answer, is *yes*, then congratulations! If not, then <u>why</u>?

Did someone tell you that you do not possess *leadership qualities*, or did you make that assumption? A word of caution, be careful who you allow to speak into your life. Some people will categorize you (with their words) from a negative perspective. If you are not careful, their perception can define you, your ambitions, and your degree of success. You can limit yourself based on declarations spoken over you. However, you have the power and authority to reject that thinking. "As a man thinketh in his heart, so is he..." (Proverbs 23:7, KJV). Therefore, how you respond to the leadership question above depends upon your definition of leadership, the characteristics that you believe leaders possess, and your perception of you.

What is Leadership?

Libraries are replete with books on the subject of leadership. Former President Harry S. Truman wrote, "Leadership is the art of getting people to do what they might not otherwise do, and to like it." Warren Bennis defines leadership as "the capacity to translate vision into reality." In 1999, Ken Blanchard said, "leadership is not something you do to people. It is something you do with people." Although the definitions may vary, in the final analysis, it takes a *leader* to execute leadership. However, for an effective leader to exercise quality leadership, the leader must establish the vision, communicate its purpose, and empower the people to make the vision a reality.

After examining much of the literature, I elected to define leadership as, *"the ability to influence the behavior of others to the extent that they are willing to engage in activities that promote accomplishment of the companies' mutual goals and objectives."* According to renowned international leadership expert, John C. Maxwell, "Leadership is <u>influence</u>, nothing more and nothing less." As a certified John C. Maxwell Leadership Team (JMT) speaker, coach, and trainer, I support this assessment 100 percent. Having the ability to influence, motivate, or change another's behavior to achieve a common goal is the ultimate objective. This is part of what

I describe as the credence test in leadership. If a leader is unable to influence his or her team, then what degree of leadership is occurring? Is the leader making a difference?

For example, when I coached the women's military post level basketball team in Korea, there were many times when we were considered the "underdog." Winning against some of our staunchest opponents was going to be impossible. Yet, through solid leadership, motivation, hard work, and a lot of practice, we won games that defied logic. Yet, we had built a solid team. Therefore, we took advantage of the odds that were against us, and turned them into opportunities for success. Although there are various styles of leadership (e.g. transformational, transactional, autocratic, democratic, situational, participative, blended), the acid test for every leader—in the end, is accomplishment of the mission.

Leadership Potential

What is potential? I recently interviewed someone who said, "Potential is a nebulous word—difficult to describe, but I know it when I see it." What a profound statement. I recall a military general making a similar statement about leadership. However, since the primary focus of this book is releasing one's leadership potential, let's examine Webster's definition of potential. Webster defines potential as something that can be developed or become actualized. For example, a gifted, talented, and disciplined athlete has the *potential* to achieve greatness in their chosen sport. However, it requires continuous training, commitment, and dedication to the sport. When I think of Olympic athletes and the degree of training they have endured for years, I marvel at their accomplishments. Somewhere in their history, a parent, coach, or teacher recognized their potential for greatness and encouraged them to pursue their dream.

Leadership Myth: Are Leaders Born or Made?

This colossal question will go down in history. For years, leadership theorists postulated that leaders possessed certain traits. They depicted key behaviors, or responded to situations in a way that characterized leadership. However, as time progressed, paradigm shifts began to occur in the thinking of many theorists and this ancient question was becoming less relevant.

Examples abound of individuals who have debunked this myth. For example, if one reviewed the pedigree of President Abraham Lincoln, no one would have imagined that he would become the sixteenth president of the United States. Although President Lincoln grew up in poverty, he did not allow the poverty to define the leader that he would one day become. Prior to winning the presidency, Lincoln ran for public office on several occasions winning and losing elections along the journey. Proving that determination and tenacity can influence outcomes, President Lincoln finally won his quest for the presidency. Today, he is revered as one of the greatest presidents of all time.

A New Leadership Perspective

What would happen if the question surrounding one's leadership lineage, ancestry, or heredity became a moot point? In other words, what positive outcomes would occur if organizations would change their perspective on the demographics of the employee and begin focusing on the leadership potential residing in that employee? Unfortunately, I have worked in several organizations where some employees were relegated to performing certain mundane tasks because they were not deemed "leadership material." Although some of these individuals were college graduates and capable of "leading," they were being judged prior to ever given the opportunity to take a leadership position. This pattern of *leadership development exclusiveness* disturbed me, because I have witnessed many individuals without prior leadership experience excel. They triumphed against the odds. Therefore, organizations *destined to win* must invest in leadership developmental programs that maximize employee productivity without reserving these programs for a "select few."

Effective leaders must be able to create an inclusive workplace that promotes the development of the entire team. Leveraging the skills and talents of team members is a business best practice. However, when organizations fail to develop their employees, money is essentially being left on the table. Untapped leadership talent now becomes a game changer. Imagine the depth and breadth of experience that these individuals can bring to the organization; yet, their leadership potential is being stifled and undeveloped. With no place to grow or go, these individuals will eventually depart for greater challenges and leadership opportunities. High turnover rates coupled with the costs associated with replacing the employees will now affect the company's profit margin. Therefore, as organizations continue to restructure due to downsizing, outsourcing, sequestration, etc., it is essential that they maximize that hidden leadership potential within their employees. Develop a leadership growth plan that will enable the individual to take their skills and talents to the next level. This definitive or decisive action will prove productive for both the company and the employee. Although there are different intrinsic and extrinsic factors that motivate employees, if someone is seeking to develop their leadership skills, then helping them to meet that need is an organization's positive investment in human capital development.

CHAPTER SUMMARY

There is no *one* definitive definition of leadership. For years, leadership theorists have penned numerous definitions focusing on the leader, follower, and situation. However, one common denominator is always present. It is the leader's ability to exert influence.

Organizations must refrain from focusing simply on a person' pedigree in determining whether an individual has the capacity to lead. There are hidden leadership gems all around us. Unfortunately, there are remnants of people today who believe that if you are born into a certain family, then you automatically possess an undeniable degree of leadership potential. Although there is a certain degree of truth to this assumption resulting from business exposure and leadership training, this is not inclusive.

History records the accomplishments of many leaders who rose to prominence not because of lineage but passion, hard work, faith, and determination. Therefore, in order to expand the leadership pool of the future, organizations must invest in individuals that have leadership potential, but may require a mentor, coach, or just an *opportunity* to execute their skills.

Organizations destined to survive in the 21st century will view this as a human capital investment and not a liability.

ॐ

"Recognize and embrace the leadership potential that is inside of you so that you can reach the destination that is before you."

—*Dr. Mary M. Gillam*

ॐ

CHAPTER 2

Uncommon Leaders: Triumph Against the Odds

T he chronicles of history document the exploits of many leaders. There are those who by birth were destined for leadership roles while others had leadership opportunities thrust upon them. Some (i.e. entrepreneurs) have even created their own leadership opportunities. Yet, there are many in whom society would have never envisioned becoming leaders. They did not have the right pedigree, education, social standing or cultural background.

The first example that I would like to discuss under the heading of *uncommon leader* is our founding president and war hero, General George Washington. This may appear as a shock, but let me explain. As a student of history and a retired military officer, I studied the life and accomplishments of General George Washington for years.

However, it was not until recently that I read or recalled General Washington's lack of a *former education* past the age of 12. In addition, he did not have any formal military training prior to becoming a British officer. Although his father was a prominent man, when he died, things changed financially for the younger Washington. He eventually had to quit school. Although he was not poor, he still had to work hard to compensate for the lack of education. Yet, he continued to learn via other methods. He would eventually become an outstanding surveyor and farmer. Having a keen interest in the military, Washington was later granted the privilege to assume his older brother's military commission after his death.   Destined for greatness, Washington received a commission as a British soldier.

As history records, General Washington proved to be a leader's leader. Images of the general crossing the Delaware River, along with him knelling down to pray, will forever be engraved in my memory. He was indeed a fascinating figure to study. Yet, no one would have ever envisioned that the general with no formal education or training, would achieve the level of success that he did. His accomplishments on the battlefield would later parlay him into becoming the nation's founding president. As the first president, Washington established the foundation upon which this nation exists today. General Washington was indeed an uncommon leader who triumphed against the odds.

From the Hood to the Hill, is the superb autobiography of Rear Admiral (Retired) Barry Black – an extraordinary leader. Admiral Black was the first African American to become the 62nd

Chaplain of the United States Senate and to serve as the Navy's Chief of Chaplains. In his autobiography, Chaplain Black describes how he overcame his humble beginnings in Baltimore, Maryland and credits his accomplishments to consistent prayer, faith, and hard work.

As I read the book, I was intrigued by Rear Admiral Black's story. For example, he was one of *eight* children. He grew up in public housing with a single, God-fearing mother. Given his humble beginnings, who would have ever imagined that he would have (1) obtained the rank of Rear Admiral, (2) became the 62nd Chaplain of the United States Senate, and (3) served as the Navy's Chief of Chaplains? He was definitely an uncommon leader who triumphed against the odds. God knew what was residing inside of Admiral Black – just like He knows the leadership potential that is lying dormant inside of us.

The two previous examples exemplify why I wrote this book. I believe that there is a measure of leadership potential inside all of us. What we do to cultivate and develop that potential is up to us. However, it may require additional training, learning, passion, faith, commitment, motivation, or just simply an opportunity.

Having been raised by my God-fearing paternal grandmother, Mrs. Lubertha Strickland Monk in a small town in Sampson County, North Carolina, I definitely understand humble beginnings. Can you imagine having married at the tender age of **14**, given birth to **17** children, widowed at the age of **48** with five teenage children still at home? If that is not enough, you are later given sole responsibility for **four** grandchildren all under the age of **six**.

That is the story of my grandmother, because that is exactly what happened to her. Yet, despite all of those difficult and painful circumstances, she never gave up. She was truly an uncommon leader and my hero because I was one of those *grandchildren* that she raised.

When I was five years old, my parents divorced. Realizing that she could no longer care for us, my mother (in her early twenties) made the painful decision to give my three siblings and me to my paternal grandmother. Although my grandmother did not have much, and would eventually go **blind** from sugar diabetes, what she had was an abundance of love for four little grandchildren who desperately needed a home.

A widow with a plethora of responsibilities, my grandmother somehow found the *strength, courage, faith, and will* to not only raise her own children, but to later raise many of her grandchildren. Her unwavering faith in God, made this possible. Despite her limited education, she was very wise. She instilled in my siblings and me life lessons that enabled us to become productive citizens in society. In her own way, my grandmother was an uncommon leader who triumphed against the odds.

My grandmother represented tenacity taken to the nth degree. Her parents died when she was a little girl; therefore, she had to grow up extremely fast. With no more than a fourth grade education, my grandmother implanted in all of us the importance of education, and the value of hard work. She would constantly remind my three siblings and me that no matter where you come from, you can be whatever you want to be in life if you are willing to work hard, and put God first. Before she went blind, she actually attended night school so that she could advance her education.

A woman of wisdom, she made a tremendous difference in my life. Many of the life principles that she taught me as a child enabled me to develop my personal and professional leadership philosophy. Given my background and humble beginnings, who would have ever predicted that I, a little girl from Roseboro, North Carolina would become a *leader* in the United States Air Force? I would advance through the ranks and achieve the rank of Colonel.

To put things in perspective, it is important to understand the demographics of the Air Force, which have not changed extensively since my retirement. According to the Department of Defense Air Force Personnel Center in December 2013, the Air Force active duty composition is as follows:

a. 325,952 Total Active Duty (18.9% are women)
b. 64,104 Officers (19.9% are women)
c. 261,748 Enlisted (18.7% are women)

As noted above, 19.9% of officers are women ranging from second lieutenant to general. Yet, the percentage of females serving at the higher military grades decreases as the rank increases. Therefore, I was blessed and honored to *earn* the rank of Colonel.

Headquarters
United States European Command
Office of the Chief of Staff
Unit 30400
APO AE 09131
21 January 2004

Lt Col Mary M. Gillam
HQ USEUCOM/ECJ5
Unit 30400
APO AE 09131

Dear Lieutenant Colonel Gillam,

Congratulations on your selection for promotion to Colonel. It is an obvious reflection of the Air Force's confidence in both your outstanding performance and great leadership potential. You are exceptionally deserving of this significant opportunity for professional growth.

My very best wishes to you for continued success, good health and happiness.

Sincerely,

JOHN B. SYLVESTER
Lieutenant General, USA
Chief of Staff

I

Figure 2: Congratulatory Note to Colonel

Yet, my military career was not without challenges. When I first entered the military, there were some individuals who held the opinion that women should not be in the Armed Forces, no less leading troops.

Figure 3: Captain Mary M. Gillam

However, this was **not** the Air Force's view, but their personal beliefs. Unfortunately, some of their behaviors reflected their personal beliefs.

For example, during my earlier years, there were those who questioned my leadership potential in light of my male counterparts. Although we had both successfully completed the same military career field training, there was no basis for differentiation except for my gender. On one occasion, I recall being assigned responsibility for all of the *support* functions, while my male colleague was given all of the *operational* related responsibilities. Despite these professional development obstacles, I was undeterred, because I knew the leadership potential that God had placed within me.

While we were both the same rank and new to the organization, it was obvious to me that the boss was making a blatant distinction between the two of us. When I brought the matter to his attention, it was ignored. Therefore, I did my job (as assigned) to the best of my ability. However, when the opportunity arose for me to rotate to a new assignment, I volunteered to go where my skills would be utilized for maximum productivity. In the previous job, I was an action officer. In my next assignment, I became the branch chief. Sometimes, it pays to pursue higher levels of responsibilities.

My goal for joining the Air Force was not to be the best female military officer, but to be the best officer that I could be, based on my leadership, management, and technical competencies. No stranger to hard work, I knew

Figure 4: Colonel Mary M. Gillam

that my work ethic, commitment to excellence, and my faith would eventually pay off, and it did.

In addition to advancing through the ranks, I was selected to attend several professional military education schools to include the Naval War College in Newport, Rhode Island. As an Air Force officer, attendance at the Navy's senior service school was significant, because not everybody gets this opportunity. Since continuous education was a major factor in the military, I also earned several advanced degrees from civilian institutions, and several graduate level certificates. When not deployed, I took advantage of the military tuition assistance benefits and spent many evenings in *night school* continuing my education earning both technical and managerial level degrees. Since I was in a technical career field (that changed constantly), I applied much of the academic education and training to my military occupation. A word to the wise—continuous learning is a best practice.

After retiring from the Air Force, and working as a government contractor, I was given the opportunity to assume another high-level leadership position. I was selected for the Senior Executive Service (SES) Corps. As an SES, my job was at the Office of the Secretary of Defense in the Pentagon, where I served as the Director of Technology, Innovation and Engineering. Since I value people and technology, this proved to be a great opportunity for me. However, after experiencing the entrepreneurial bug, I decided to take another leadership leap of faith and start my own consulting firm. With over 30+ years working in technology, leadership, and management, my goal was to create a business that reflected my value system, ethics, and hard work.

Having won numerous military and civic leadership awards, many people have referred to me as an "uncommon leader who triumphed against the odds." However, any degree of success that I have experienced, I not only credit it to my faith in God, but also to my loving grandmother. She was the catalyst that taught me to believe that I could rise above my humble beginnings, activate my passion for success, and release my leadership potential.

While in the military, I traveled extensively around the world. In some countries, I witnessed unbelievable poverty. I will admit that I have yet to see in the United States the level of poverty that I observed in these countries. Therefore, I do not dwell on my humble beginnings. My goal is to encourage and inspire individuals to become the best that God created them to become.

Transform your thinking so that you can go beyond where you are today. Envision yourself where you want to be in the future. I am convinced that if I could do it by the grace of God, then so can you. This is why I am passionate about helping others to grow and develop their leadership potential. There is nothing stopping you. Take action today and decide within yourself to become the uncommon leader that others will want to follow.

CHAPTER SUMMARY

Uncommon leaders have been prevalent throughout history. Many people have risen above humble beginnings and have triumphed against the odds. Leadership potential is not relegated to where you come from, but rather what you do with the opportunities you receive. When opportunity knocks at your door, what will you do?

ॐ

CHAPTER 3

Leadership Characteristics that People Value

S ocial scientists and leadership theorists have studied leadership characteristics for years. Are there specific characteristics that correlate with effective leadership? In order to identify leadership potential in others, it is important to understand what leadership characteristics people value. What characteristics remain at the forefront of effective leadership?

In addressing these questions, I partnered with an independent survey agency to collect some informal data on understanding leadership potential. An anonymous survey was conducted using random sampling and a mixture of open and closed-ended questions. The purpose of the survey was to explore the perceptions of a diverse group of individuals regarding their perspectives on leadership potential. The participants (from across the United States) range from 18-65 years of age. Although a sample size of 150 was originally selected, 170 people participated in the survey. Of the 170 participants, 97 (57.1%) were men and 73 (42.9%) were female. Regarding education, 126 (74.0%) had a college degree, 35 (20.7%) had some college, and 9 (5.3%) had no degree.

Characteristics of an Effective Leader

Respondents were asked a series of questions. In the next few paragraphs, I will briefly discuss some of the questions. The respondents were asked, "What are the characteristics of an effective leader?" Appendix 2 contains a detailed listing of the responses. As I analyzed the contents of the responses, several characteristics begin to emerge. They are:

- Ability to inspire, motivate, charismatic, passionate about the job.
- Set good example for others to emulate.
- Great communicator and listener.
- Servant leader attitude; high emotional intelligence
- Visionary, thought-provoking.
- Integrity, honesty, respectful, humble, approachable, trust worthy, fair.
- Gives credit to others; open to ideas, team player, and ability to delegate.
- Life-long learner, intelligent, critical-thinker.
- Decision-maker, takes charge, strong-presence, well-qualified for the position.

The above descriptors depict some of the characteristics that people value in leaders. As documented in numerous studies, the ability to lead encompasses many attributes. Developing these skills requires commitment and determination. Therefore, if you aspire to lead, spend time reviewing these characteristics. How many of them do you currently possess?

Importance of Developing Leadership Potential

During the survey, respondents were also asked, "How important is it to develop your leadership potential?" Of the 170 responses, 53 people (31.2%) thought that it was extremely important. Fifty-two people (30.6%) believed it was very important. Forty-two people (24.7%) considered it moderately important. Eleven people (6.5%) thought it was slightly important, and 12 people (7.1%) commented that it was not important. Of note, 86 (51.5%) of the participants were introverts and 81 (48.5%) were extroverts.

Degree of Leadership Training

Respondents were also asked, "How would you describe your leadership skills?" Of the 170 respondents, eight people (4.7%) stated they were extremely well trained. Fifty-nine people

(34.9%) were very well trained. Seventy-one people (42.0%) were moderately trained. Twenty-three people (13.6%) were slightly trained, and eight people (4.27%) had no leadership training.

Why is this data significant? As companies strive to streamline operations, it is imperative that employees continue to add value to their organizations. By expanding one's ability to accomplish a myriad of duties (i.e. assume a team leadership role), it can broaden your job prospects within the organization. In addition, developing your leadership skills will offer a greater degree of employee flexibility and diversity.

Leadership Potential & Promotion Opportunity

In addition to the above questions, respondents were asked, "Does developing one's leadership potential influence future promotion opportunities?" Appendix 3 contains the data from the survey. Of the 170 participants in the survey, 146 answered the question. The majority of the respondents replied "yes." Below are some of their responses.

- Yes, being able to lead should help increase your opportunities.
- Yes, employees want people who are able to take charge of a group and run a project.
- If someone is well versed in leading and dealing with others, they can often transfer these skills to other jobs.
- Yes, definitely. My MBA was instrumental in my promotion at work.
- I believe it does. A leader is someone who goes beyond what is required. If an employee is not wanting to go the extra mile, then he/she will not be an effective leader.
- Yes, someone with greater drive and initiative is bound to be promoted more quickly.
- A trained leader can utilize their maximum potential.
- Yes, a company can see that an employee is striving for leadership and

looking for greater challenges in the workplace.
- Yes. Many places seem to be lacking trained leaders and managers and I feel as if most places would welcome trained leaders with open arms. Without proper management and leadership, the workforce can significantly suffer.

Passion, Cause and Leadership

During the survey, respondents were also asked, "Can activating one's passion concerning a particular cause motivate an individual to step out of their comfort zone and assume a leadership role regarding that cause?" Appendix 5 contains the detailed data. Some of the most interesting responses are below.

- Yes, *passion* can be a powerful tool for a leader. I have seen people who I would not characterize as leaders *transform into strong leaders* when they have been faced with a cause they suddenly related to.
- People who have no great desire for leadership may be eager and effective

leaders in areas they are passionate about. An example would be *fundraising for a disease* that has affected someone close to them.

- Yes. I know from personal experience that I would step up in more of a leadership role on something that I am super passionate about rather than something I do not know much about.

- Yes. I work with the homeless, and have assumed a leadership position in my organization because I am *able to overcome my fears* to better serve the people we work with.

- Yes. Giving someone an *opportunity* to prove themselves in a situation that is more desirable or passionate for them, gives them confidence to take on more difficult situations.

- Absolutely. Often times when a person is *dedicated to a cause*, they will take command to make sure certain actions occur.

- Yes, passion can allow a person to overlook their natural reservation or lack of self-confidence and be an effective leader.

- Yes. I have *experienced this first-hand, when I took leadership of a group because no one else was willing to.* It was my passion for this thing that made me realized that I had to do something to encourage its growth.
- Absolutely, it is easier to lead in a situation that a person is passionate about because that is a big motivator and there is a much stronger desire to do well and have those you lead do well.
- Yes. I think *a cause that one believes in will motivate* one where in different circumstances one may decline the leadership role if they have no strong belief one way or the other.
- Yes. If people are passionate about a certain area then it would cause them to go outside their comfort zone.
- Yes. Being passionate about something can diminish or eliminate self-consciousness or self-doubt.
- Yes. If someone is normally reluctant to lead but has a burning desire for a particular "cause" they step forward.
- Yes, *passion will push you past your boundaries.*

- Yes. Being an introvert, I know that if I am passionate enough about something I will want to be involved even if it makes me a bit uncomfortable.
- Passion can be a driving force for change including finding leaders where there was no plan prior to it.
- Yes, if an individual has a personal goal or "cause" they often are more comfortable or confident in leading others concerning the subject.
- I absolutely believe that passion influences leadership. .. Even introverts like myself jump up to lead in situations that we are passionate about.
- Yes. Passion about a cause means you are willing to do what you can to help the cause. If you are brave enough, this can mean taking on a leadership role.

- Although the survey instrument was limited, there is evidence to substantiate the assertion that being passionate about a cause can produce hidden leaders. Since this is part of the premise behind the CORE Leadership Development Model, the overwhelming positive response rate to the question was enlightening.

Response to a Leadership Opportunity

Respondents were also asked, "When assessing leadership potential, does a person's response to a leadership opportunity reveal information about that individual's desire to lead?" Appendix 4 contains responses to this question. Some of the key responses are below.

- Yes, if a person does not take opportunities to lead, there may not be a desire to be a leader. There may be the *fears associated with being the leader*.
- Yes. Those seeking to develop and improve their own leadership abilities *show a desire to want to lead*, and are good leaders.
- Some people are *just waiting for the opportunity*; others *create their own opportunities*, and a few just need to be put in a position where they find that out about themselves.
- Definitely. Leaders are eager to take on leadership opportunities and if a person does not seem excited by the opportunity, they will most likely lack the passion (although not necessarily

the skills) required to be an effective leader.

- Yes, declining a leadership opportunity might be taken as a lack of desire. It could also be based on other factors such as a recognition that the particular opportunity was not one for which the person selected was qualified.

- Of course. If I decline an opportunity or do a half-hearted job, I don't desire a leadership position. However, this is something that needs to be evaluated on a regular basis – just because I wasn't ready for a position last year doesn't' mean I don't feel I am ready now.

- Yes, it does. If one tries to reason why they are not a good fit for the position or that they'd rather stay where they are, then they are probably right. Just stay. However, if they instead seek the leadership opportunity challenge, educate themselves on any knowledge / experience shortfalls, and make that job their own, there is almost no way to fail. Positive attitudes are contagious and our best leaders lead by example.

- Yes, if given the chance, most people who want to lead will jump at the chance.

- How a person responds to a leadership opportunity can accelerate or derail one's career. The majority of the respondents asserted that emerging leaders would respond to the opportunity in the affirmative. Although there may be some internal/external factors to prevent acceptance of a leadership opportunity, the data revealed that to be (in some cases) a small outlier.

Evaluate and Learn

While in the military, it was routine practice for organizations to conduct "deep dive" reviews after each deployment and exercise. Lessons learned were essential to our improving our tactics, techniques, and procedures for future operations. During the survey, respondents were asked, "How important is it for a leader to evaluate their performance following a leadership activity?" Seventy-three people (44.0%) indicated extremely important. Sixty-nine people (41.6%) recorded very important while 21 people (12.7%) indicated moderately important.

Leadership Development Programs

When asked if organizations should have programs to encourage their staff to develop their leadership potential, 158 people (92.9%) of the respondents replied yes, while 12 people (7.1%) answered no.

Respondents were also asked, "How receptive would you be in using a simple, easy-to-use leadership development model to help you discover your leadership potential?' Thirty people (18.2%) were extremely receptive. Sixty-eight people (41.2%) were very receptive. Forty-five people (27.3%) replied moderately receptive, while 7 people (4.2%) replied slightly receptive.

CHAPTER SUMMARY

In this chapter, we reviewed research from an independent survey distributed to individuals across the United States. The purpose of the survey was to explore the perceptions of a diverse group of individuals regarding their perspectives on developing leadership potential. Participants were asked a series of questions. The majority of the research data reinforces the premise for my development of the CORE Leadership Development Model. Using random sampling and a mixture of open and closed-ended questions, the data provided a substantial degree of confidence in the CORE proposition.

In the next section of the book, we will explore the different parts of the CORE Leadership Development Model. Each aspect of the model is presented in separate chapters. Numerous examples coupled with personal experiences are used to reinforce the model's concepts. Thought-provoking questions are also used to underpin the discussion.

ॐ

PART II

Understanding the CORE Leadership Development Model

- ✓ Is Fear Jeopardizing Your Career?

- ✓ What Cause Will Drive You to Act?

- ✓ What Happens When Opportunity Knocks?

- ✓ Where is Your Leadership Response Meter?

- ✓ Evaluate and Learn

ॐ

CHAPTER 4

Is Fear Jeopardizing Your Career?

I magine this scenario. The boss walks into the office and exclaims, "Team—given our specialized core competencies and expertise, we have the opportunity to significantly grow our business. There is a big proposal on the table, and we can capture the work. However, I need someone to take the leadership reins of this project as soon as possible." After contemplating the request, *no* team member readily steps forward. Can you picture the surprise on the face of the boss?

Although this is a hypothetical example, I would postulate that it is not impossible. Let me ask, "Have you ever experienced or witnessed the above scenario?" If your answer is yes, there were probably a myriad of reasons why the *project lead position* remained vacant. Would you agree that **fear** may have hindered some of the team members from stepping forward?

At one time or another, we have all experienced this sentiment. Despite having the skill and talent to lead the project, we surrender to our fear. Unfortunately, we sometimes doubt our abilities, leaving the boss to look elsewhere for leadership.

As we explore this discussion further, we are confronted with the fact that the above hypothetical example represents only one side of the story. For example, within some organizations, there are individuals who appear to be natural-born leaders. They exhibit the behavioral and trait characteristics associated with leaders. Likewise, they appear to have found their niche or passion and lead effortlessly. They are not afraid to step forward and embrace new challenges. Despite their abilities and successes, there are just as many people in organizations who have yet to *discover and release* their leadership potential. In many instances, these individuals are *gifted* with exceptional ability. As a result, these individuals represent the target audience in which the *CORE Leadership Development Model* was designed.

Having spent over 30+ years working in telecommunications and information technology in the military, government and the corporate sector, I recognize the need for continuous leadership development. As a military leader, I was expected to step forward and take charge. On many occasions, I had to step out of my "comfort zone" and lead the team. For example, during my first command tour, I deployed my entire squadron to Egypt. Given the cultural differences and language barriers, I was still responsible for ensuring the well-being of my team, and that the mission was accomplished. As I mentioned in a previous chapter, that is the ultimate responsibility of the leader. Formal leadership and management training was a core competency within my organizations.

Yet, there are many reasons why talented individuals in organizations may choose not to assume a leadership position. One prominent reason is fear of failure. For example, one may ask, "Although I have the talent and skills to lead this project, what will happen if I am not successful and fail?" While this question and emotion is understandable, it can limit one's ability to embrace the unknown. Success can be one passion point away from one's decision to step forward. However, you will never know if success was within reach if you allow fear to deprive you of your leadership potential.

In his book, *Leading Leaders to Leadership: 21 Secrets for Leveraging Your Way to greater Success*, international bestselling author John

Fuhrman made a profound statement about failure. He wrote, "Those who risk failure courageously put their best efforts into the preparation stage and take action as soon as possible." I am reminded of a passage in Second Timothy in which the Apostle Paul writes to Timothy, "For this reason, I remind you to keep alive the gift that God gave you...for the Spirit that God has given us does not make us timid, instead, his Spirit fills us with power, love, and self-control" (2 Timothy 1:6-7, GNT). Paul cautions Timothy to not allow the gift that he has been given to die.

In retrospect, what gifts are you allowing to die within you? What impediments are hindering you from becoming the leader that you were destined to be? Are these external obstacles are internal impediments?

CHAPTER SUMMARY

Having suffered from fear of heights, I can attest that fear can be an emotional giant.

However, it is not until you *face* the giant, that you achieve the victory. Let me share a personal example. When I received my military assignment to Utah, I never thought that the gigantic mountain passes would prove a challenge for me. Since I did not grow up in mountainous terrain, I never had to deal with them. Yet, I knew that I had to gain the victory over this situation.

When I received my assignment to Oklahoma, I knew that this would be the test. Based on the route that I was taking, I had to cross numerous mountain passes. What worked for me is my faith. I prayed and asked God to deliver me from the crippling fear that I experienced when I traveled over the mountains to Utah. He answered my prayer. I drove to Oklahoma and knew that I had experienced the victory. For me, it was truly a miracle because I kept my mind focused on God. The trip to Oklahoma was one of the most calming and peaceful trips I had ever experienced.

In summary, fear can undoubtedly jeopardize and impede an individual from developing their leadership potential. Although a certain degree of fear is understandable, I caution you not to allow it to rob you of success in your personal, spiritual, or professional life. I encourage you to face the giant and unleash the leadership potential that is resident inside of you.

ও

Understanding the 4 Step Model

✓ *CAUSE*
✓ OPPORTUNITY
✓ RESPONSE
✓ EVALUATION

ॐ

CHAPTER 5

What Cause Will Drive You to Act?

O ne of the most profound attributes a leader can possess is passion. Are you passionate about what you are doing? This correlation is not new. Many scholars have recorded the importance of passion in describing leadership. As reflected in the survey, numerous respondents indicated that *passion for a cause* can influence a person's decision to assume a leadership role. Passion and commitment can motivate leaders to step forward and continue the charge. When authentic, a leader's passion can permeate throughout the entire organization.

Having a **cause** that stimulates your passion is the **first step** in understanding the CORE Leadership Development Model. Ask yourself, "Is there a cause that would motivate you to step out of your comfort zone and assume a leadership role?"

Find a Cause

When I was a sophomore in college, I never imagine running for a seat on the student government council. Although I had served on the student council in high school, I had no plans to run for office in college. Yet, after listening to several students voice their opinions about things that required change, I decided to throw my hat in the ring and run for office. Since I shared some of the same concerns with the students, I developed a passion for the *cause* and it became my platform. After running a successful campaign, I won the election serving as the vice president of the sophomore class.

Now, let's look at a more intriguing example of how a cause can drive you to action. How many of you have heard of Candy Lightner? If not, let me share with you tidbits of her story. Lightner is the founding president and _mother_ who started the nonprofit organization, Mothers Against Drunk Driving (MADD). Motivated by a horrific tragedy that her family endured, Lightner chose to take action. Experiencing the tragic loss of her 13-year-old daughter to a drunk driver, gave Lightner unfortunately a **cause** for which she would create lasting change.

Imagine the heartache and pain that this mother experienced. Losing a child can be one of the most heart wrenching events a parent could ever experience. Rallying others who had endured similar tragedies, Lightner championed a cause that would change America. Out of her pain was born an organization that today is the largest nonprofit dedicated to **preventing drunk driving and underage drinking**.

Lightner's determination to influence legislation in this area was a cause worth fighting. Although, she has since departed MADD, Lightner's name will forever be associated with a movement that has made a positive different in our nation today. Lightner proved that one woman's commitment to a cause can make a positive difference and become the agent for change.

Other prominent non-profit organizations that are driven by major causes are the American Diabetes Association, and the Susan G. Komen Foundation for breast cancer awareness. I mention these organizations because they both have unfortunately impacted my family. My grandmother lost her eyesight due to the effects of diabetes. Breast cancer claimed the lives of several of my relatives. When it comes to developing one's leadership abilities, these organizations and others create numerous opportunities for people around the country to get involved even at the grass roots or baseline level. From orchestrating fundraisers to organizing local races, the opportunities are boundless. Find a cause that you are passionate about and get involved.

Commitment to a *cause* is one of the primary reasons I joined the military. I took an oath stating that I would support and defend the constitution of the United States against all enemies, foreign and domestic. Passion for this cause enabled me to lead several organizations by training and preparing for the mission at hand.

In 1991, I deployed to Ankara, Turkey as part of the National Military Intelligence Support Team. This was during the critical early days of Operation Provide Comfort, which was the Kurdish Humanitarian Relief Effort. This was a very tense situation. Although my family was afraid for my safety (especially since armed terrorists were active in that region of the country), I was committed to the cause for which I had raised my hand. Having been trained to carry out the mission, I was determined to fulfill my responsibilities and those of my team.

In support of the Haitian humanitarian relief effort in 1994, I deployed to Guantanamo (GITMO) Bay, Cuba. As the Director for Command, Control, Communications, and Computer (C4) Systems for the Air Force Element, I worked through some difficult challenges to get the necessary deployable C4 equipment to support the operation. Despite the obstacles, I was not going to give up. The cause that we were tasked to support was too great. By teaming with other deployable units in the region, my team and I was able to get the equipment required and complete the mission.

In keeping with the military theme, let's take a look at a very familiar biblical example involving David and Goliath. In 1 Samuel chapter 16, we find the story of David, the youngest of eight sons born to Jesse. David was a shepherd who spent his time caring for his father's sheep. This is a fascinating story because we find that leadership is not relegated to age. While caring for the sheep, David was entrusted with his family's livelihood. As shepherds, they relied on the sheep trade for income. Even in this instance, David was learning management and responsibility.

As history records, Goliath was the Philistine champion warrior. He was over nine feet tall. Realizing that the Israelites were no match for them, the Philistines gathered together to do battle against the armies of Israel. In that day, there was no man (in his own strength) capable of defeating Goliath. Because of this dilemma, Goliath laughed at the Israelite warriors. For fun, Goliath would challenge the men of Israel to come out and battle him. If Israel was able to defeat the Philistines, then the Philistines would become servants to Israel. However, if the Philistines prevailed, then the Israelites would serve them. Israel's freedom was on the line. Yet, all of the men of Israel feared Goliath—but not David, the future Israelite king. In his boldness, David declares, "Is there not a *cause* [worth fighting]?" (1 Samuel 17:29, KJV)

David immediately recognized the severity of the situation. He was fighting for Israel's freedom. Although he was a mere shepherd boy, David recognized the **cause** that ignited his passion. He took advantage of the opportunity and exercised history-making leadership.

Having a cause in which you are passionate about can motivate you to take action. As in David's case, his cause provided him with an unexpected leadership opportunity. I propose that if there is a cause in which you are passionate, it can stir up the gift that God has placed inside of you. So, what is holding you back?

CHAPTER SUMMARY

If you desire to develop your leadership skills, find a **"cause"** that stimulates your passion point. Get involved at the grassroots level. Engage in a cause that is worthy of your time, talent, resources, and energy. Seek out a leadership opportunity associated with that cause. This is a great place to develop your leadership talent.

Do not allow fear, complacency, or contentment to deprive you from achieving the greatness that God has for you. Sometimes, we settle for being a follower when God has placed inside of us the ability to lead. Are you willing to take the leap and become the next great leader?

❧

Understanding the 4 Step Model

✓ CAUSE
✓ *OPPORTUNITY*
✓ RESPONSE
✓ EVALUATION

ॐ

CHAPTER 6

What Happens When Opportunity Knocks?

I n the context of leadership, **opportunity** can be a funny thing. It can happen when you least expect it. Future leaders prepare and recognize when opportunity knocks at the door. Having a cause in which you are passionate can lead to an opportunity for you to get involved. This is the **second step** of the CORE Leadership Development Model.

Seek Out An Opportunity

In the early 2000s, I volunteered to organize a Women's Day Program at my local

71

church. The pastor asked someone to take on the challenge, so I volunteered. Given the amount of work required (i.e. keynote speaker, music, dinner, fundraiser), I knew that this would be a great opportunity to continue to develop my leadership skills. Since the ladies and I decided to do a skit as part of the program, time management was critical. From rehearsals to costumes, we had to plan for every aspect of the program. In the end, the Women's Day Program was a great success. Although this is a simple example, the purpose is to show you how you can engage in a leadership opportunity and continue to grow as a leader. If you are determined to develop your leadership skills, there are numerous opportunities to get involved.

Ray Kroc epitomizes what it means to seek out a leadership opportunity and make history. Kroc was already an experienced leader, but he undoubtedly saw an opportunity with the McDonald brothers and chose to act. Although he did not bear the McDonald name, he recognized the value of the McDonald restaurant chain. In 1955, Kroc established the McDonald's Corporation. Since its inception, the company has experienced continual growth. The McDonald's golden arch is undeniably one of the most recognizable symbols in the world. Five years after creating the corporation, Kroc bought the exclusive rights to the name. Recognizing the genius in franchises, Kroc created a legacy in which entrepreneurs around the world have invested in the McDonald's brand. By adhering to standardized business practices in a variety of areas to include food quality, value, infrastructure, apparel, training, etc., McDonald's customers worldwide can expect the highest degree of quality and service.

Let's look at another example of a team of individuals who recognized a leadership opportunity from an entrepreneurial perspective. In 2004, Mark Zuckerberg, Eduardo Saverin,

Andrew McCollum, Dustin Moskovitz, and Chris Hughes founded Facebook. Although the social media network was initially a closed network, it was later opened to include anyone over the age of 13. Facebook became one of the fastest growing social media sites in history. Using their computer skills and business savvy, the founders quickly became leaders in their industry. Having personally used Facebook, Twitter, Linkedin, and Google+ to advertise my business endeavors, I applaud the work of the founders of each of these platforms.

Sometimes leadership opportunities occur unexpectedly. For example, while serving as an International Political Military Affairs Officer in the military, I had the opportunity to accompany a senior United States senator to various countries in Africa. Although this was a high-profile trip, it was very short notice. Since the trip occurred during a holiday weekend, much of the government staff was unavailable. My boss began a series of phone calls trying to reach someone to travel with the senator. Although I was not the primary action officer for these particular countries, I was knowledgeable enough of the region that I felt comfortable accepting this opportunity.

The lesson that I learned from this engagement was that a person never knows when a leadership opportunity may present itself. Since my office had an organized system for collecting country-related data, I knew where to find the information necessary for the trip. I invested several hours getting knowledgeable on the critical topics associated with each country. Because of my willingness to accept this unexpected leadership opportunity, I got the chance to serve as an adviser to the senator on key international topics.

Let's review another example of someone who accepted a major leadership opportunity. In the first chapter of Joshua, we find that Moses had died. The next in line to assume the mantle of leadership was Joshua. God saw the leadership potential in Joshua and charged him to lead the Israelites into the Promised Land. Since Joshua had served under Moses for many years, he was intimately familiar with the "cause" or mandate that had been given to Moses. Now, the leadership opportunity to lead the people was given to Joshua.

Nehemiah is another example in whom God saw leadership potential. Although Nehemiah was serving as the cupbearer to the King of Persia, God had a greater plan for his life. He was destined to lead the Israelites in rebuilding the walls of Jerusalem. After hearing the news that the walls had been destroyed and the gates had been set on fire, Nehemiah wept and mourned for days. This area was his heritage—the resting place of his fathers. Now, it had been destroyed.

As we read the book of Nehemiah, we find that he definitely had a cause in which he had an intense passion, which was to "rebuild the walls of Jerusalem." The **opportunity** arose when Nehemiah heard that the walls were destroyed. He could have easily ignored this event and remained as the cupbearer to the King. However, deep inside, Nehemiah knew that something had to be done to restore the walls of Jerusalem, so he accepted the leadership challenge.

CHAPTER SUMMARY

If you want to develop your leadership potential, seek out opportunities to lead. If there are no opportunities available, create your own (i.e. local race, fundraiser, church function, little league coach, homeowner's association committee, city council). Volunteer to lead or chair an event that will cause you to step out of your comfort zone and take on the mantle of leadership. As presented in this chapter, there are many kinds of opportunities that you can take advantage—if you choose.

ॐ

Understanding the 4 Step Model

✓ *CAUSE*
✓ OPPORTUNITY
✓ ***RESPONSE***
✓ EVALUATION

છે

CHAPTER 7

Where is Your Leadership Response Meter?

How rich is the cemetery? Just imagine if one could develop statistics for the gifts and talents that went unclaimed by their owners. Composers died full of songs that were never written. Authors perished having never started books that were birthed inside of them. There are leaders who could have potentially changed the destiny of humankind, but they chose to ignore the leadership potential that resided in them.

The **third step** in the CORE Leadership Development Model is **response.** How one responds to an opportunity will reveal much about their desire to develop their leadership potential. I propose that the response could fall into several categories such as (1) positive, (2) negative, (3) indifferent, or (4) other (i.e. extenuating circumstance prohibiting a person from accepting the opportunity.

As recorded in the survey by many respondents, there are many drivers that can affect a person's response to a leadership opportunity. However, if there are no extenuating circumstances, then a person's response to a leadership opportunity may reflect on their desire to lead. Although a person can be passionate about a cause, and have the opportunity to act, there is no guarantee that they will *respond* favorably to the opportunity.

Respond in the Affirmative

This part of the model is interesting because it can reveal a lot about an individual's desire to lead. In chapter 4, we discussed the hypothetical example in which the boss was asking for someone to accept the role of project lead. Yet, no one came forward. As a leader, if this was reflective of my team, I would reexamine my human capital leadership development strategy to determine where my training was ineffective or missing the mark. As leaders, it is our responsibility to help develop the next generation of leaders. Encouraging individuals to develop a personal leadership growth plan is a step in the right direction. Successful leadership training is a two prone approach. Action must occur on the part of the individual as well as the organization.

If a person desires to develop their leadership skills, they have to be willing to respond positively to the leadership challenge. In chapter 6, we reviewed the story of Joshua who was chosen to replace Moses as the new leader of the Israelites. He was given the mandate to take the people over the Jordan River. Although, Joshua could have declined the assignment, he chose to *respond in the affirmative.* Joshua was a leader awaiting his opportunity. When the opportunity presented itself, Joshua was ready. His actions immediately following his selection are indicative of his preparation. For example, he commanded the people to prepare provisions, for in three days, they would pass over the Jordan River. In retrospect, Joshua was passionate about the cause; accepted the opportunity, and succeeded in leading the people across the Jordan. He proved to be a very effective leader.

Now, let me share a personal experience. Prior to starting M2G Dynamic Leadership Solutions, LLC, I served as the Director of Technology, Innovation, and Engineering at the Office of the Secretary of Defense at the Pentagon. However, when I interviewed for the position, it was actually a different job. Yet, because of my extensive technical background and leadership experience, I knew that I had the requisite skills to lead the organization. Since I was the first

Director in the position, I had to implement all of the basic organizational functions required to operate a major directorate.   I had three male division chiefs that reported directly to me. Having completed this level task on many previous occasions, I knew the degree of work required. As an experienced and seasoned leader, I accepted the leadership challenge and successfully led the organization.

Another example that I would like to discuss involves the Girl Scouts of America. When Frances Hesselbein became the CEO of the Girl Scouts, the organization was in serious trouble. The organization had experienced eight consecutive years of continuous decline in membership. Having grew up in the organization serving in various leadership roles, Hesselbein was the *right person to respond to this leadership opportunity* and takeover the organization. Her response meter was calibrated for action.   In order to survive in the 21st century, Hesselbein knew that the organization needed to change. From extending its membership to girls nationwide, to provided training that aligned with the needs of young women today, Hesselbein led the charge.

CHAPTER SUMMARY

How one responds to a leadership opportunity can reveal much about their personal perception of their ability to lead. If they are confident in their abilities, it will probably be reflected in their response. Likewise, the opposite may occur if the individual is less confident in their ability to lead.

There are many factors that can impact a person's willingness to step forward. However, if there are no extenuating circumstances, then how a person responds to a leadership opportunity can reflect on their desire to lead.

ಎ

Understanding the 4 Step Model

✓ CAUSE
✓ OPPORTUNITY
✓ RESPONSE
✓ *EVALUATION*

❧

"Uncommon leaders are all around us. Are you one of those

hidden gems?"

—*Dr. Mary M. Gillam*

૨૦

CHAPTER 8

Evaluate Your Response and Learn

T he **fourth** and final step in understanding the CORE Leadership Development Model is **evaluation**. Is evaluation important? When respondents were asked a similar question during the survey, 44 %indicated extremely important, 41.6% recorded very important while 12.7% indicated moderately important. You can have a **cause** that you are passionate about and be presented with an **opportunity** to lead. However, your **response** to the leadership opportunity is the core of the evaluation process. For example, what kind of response did you provide? Was it

(1) positive, (2) negative, (3) indifferent, or (4) other? Why did you respond that way? Are there underlying reasons that influenced your response to the leadership opportunity?

Why should you evaluate your response? First, there could be underlying reasons that are blocking your ability to grow and develop as a leader. For example, negative words spoken over you as a child may have you locked in a prism of defeat. Getting past the "I can't do it stage" may require a greater degree of training, faith, commitment, and resources far beyond the scope of this book.

Second, organizations routinely engaged in lessons learned activities to determine areas for improvement. Regardless of your response to the leadership opportunity, it is a business best practice to explore the lessons learned.

For example, if you responded positively to the questions, please take the time to answer the following questions:

1. What could I have done better?
2. What training is required to enhance my skills?
3. How did my leadership influence the team?
4. Did we meet our goal?
5. How prepared was I to accept the leadership challenge?

Likewise, if you responded negatively to the leadership opportunity, ask yourself the following questions:

1. Do I really want to develop my leadership potential? The answer to this question is critical to determining whether this exercise is for you.
2. Where there internal or external extenuating circumstances?
3. What can I do to get prepared for the next leadership opportunity?
4. Are there low scale opportunities that I can volunteer with to enhance my confidence and grow my skills?
5. Do I need to get a mentor, coach, or help from my boss to help develop my skills?

Now, let's look at a few examples that will underpin the four steps in the CORE Leadership Development Model. These are simple examples to help reiterate the basic principles of the model. In addition, the examples are used to emphasize key points.

The first example involves a woman named Deborah, who happens to be an introvert. She is the central figure in this hypothetical story. In Deborah's neighborhood, there is a local nonprofit organization interested in helping to educate the community with healthy food preparation. Given the focus on healthy living, the organization wanted to incorporate a basic cooking class for interested students. The goal was to educate students on how to prepare healthier meals versus relying on fast foods.

Because they did not have a big budget, the organization was looking initially for volunteers. Because of Deborah's reputation in the community for being an outstanding cook, her name was submitted as a candidate for the position. When asked if she would be interested in this opportunity to teach and educate the students in cooking, Deborah responded, "Yes, I would love the opportunity. Since I am *passionate about cooking*, I would love to do it. I routinely teach kids in my house, so I can develop a curriculum and begin to teach the students at your facility some very basic healthy dishes."

However, some of Deborah's friends were astonished at her willingness to lead this event. When asked why she agreed to the position, Deborah replied, "Although I am an introvert, I am passionate about cooking. It comes natural for me. **It is my gift**. Therefore, I can easily teach others about it. Since I am operating in my gift, I am comfortable leading this event."

Let's analyze this example. The breakdown analysis is as follows:

> a. First, Deborah was a great cook and an introvert.

    b. Second, the nonprofit in her neighborhood had an emergent need for a cooking instructor to lead a cooking class.

    c. Third, Deborah was presented with an opportunity that correlated with her skills and passion for cooking.

    d. Fourth, Deborah's response to this opportunity was positive.

Why is Deborah's response important? As an introvert, Deborah could have easily **refused** the opportunity. Although she was probably not a natural born leader, Deborah decided to step out from behind the veil of fear and reservation, and began to cultivate her leadership potential by starting with something that she loved. That is the key to this entire model. Begin your leadership development training by finding a cause that will drive you to action.

The next two examples reflect great biblical leaders whose initial response to a leadership opportunity was <u>not</u> proactive. For example, when Moses was initially called to deliver the Israelites, he begins to identify all of the things that would preclude him from *leading*. Although he grew up in the House of Pharaoh, Moses claimed that his speech was not eloquent. However, after exhausting his line of reasoning, Moses finally accepted the leadership challenge, and the rest is history. Moses became one of the greatest leaders of all time. From books to onscreen movies, the story of Moses has been passed down through generations. Yet, Moses initially did not see himself as a leader. How about you? Is there leadership potential inside of you?

In the next example, we find a guy, who from all accounts would probably never have been considered a leader. The story of Gideon is fascinating because Gideon did not see himself as a mighty warrior—no less a leader. Yet, in Judges 6:12, an angel of the Lord appeared to Gideon while he was at the winepress. The angel probably shocked Gideon when he said to him "The Lord is with thee, *thou mighty man of valor.*" (Judges 6:12, KJV). Gideon probably looked around and said, "who me?" God had chosen Gideon to deliver the Israelites out of the hands of the Midianites. Because of Gideon's hesitancy to step forward, he required numerous confirmations (fleeces) to ensure that he was not imagining things.

Despite Gideon's earlier hesitation, he later accepted the leadership challenge and proved to be a mighty warrior and a great leader. The story of Gideon's triumph over the Midianites is well known. With 300 men, Gideon accomplished an impossible mission. Although the Midianites had more men, armor, supplies, etc., Gideon had the King of Kings leading and directing him and his band of men.

However, Gideon's initial response to the leadership challenge is indicative of how we respond sometimes to leadership opportunities.

Although, others may see leadership potential in us, sometimes we fail to see it in ourselves.

CHAPTER SUMMARY

The purpose of this chapter was to discuss the significance of evaluating one's response to a leadership opportunity. Evaluation is a key component of the lessons learned process. What did you learn from your response? Whether the response to the leadership opportunity is positive, negative, or indifferent, it reveals critical information about the individual's desire to lead.

The final section of this book identifies how organizations can help to grow leaders from within their organizations. Through innovation and diversity, organizations can expand their leadership consortium. By building a diverse leadership team, organizations are promoting a workplace of inclusion. The message to the employee is that your voice, your opinion, your perspective counts in this organization.

PART III

Building a Diverse Leadership Team

- ✓ Growing Leaders Through

  Innovation Exploration

- ✓ Leveraging the Strength of

  Diversity and Inclusion

ॐ

CHAPTER 9

Growing Leaders through Innovation Exploration

W hat would you say if I asked you the question, "Is Innovation Dead?" Several months ago, a journalist with Help a Reporter Out.com or (HARO) actually asked that question. Intrigued and amused, I responded to the question and said, "If innovation is dead, then America is in a world of hurt."

Why did I find this question intriguing? According to a 2012 Study conducted by the Department of Commerce entitled, "The Competitiveness and Innovation Capacity of the United States, "...innovation is the key driver of competitiveness, wage and job growth, and long-term economic growth." In 2013, the United States was ranked fifth in the Global Innovation Index. However, in 2012, the United States was ranked 10th which is significant, because we made a 5-point jump. Yet, there is still more work to do because innovation is not dead.

Innovation is the *cornerstone* of continuous growth, and the engine that will revive our economy. According to President Obama, "The key to our success—as it has always been—will be to compete by developing new products, by generating new industries, by maintaining our role as the world's engine of scientific discovery and technological innovation. It's absolutely essential to our future." Yet, it will take innovative thought leaders to expand their horizons in order to energize, inspire, and galvanize their teams to become ***innovative thinkers and future leaders***.

What is Innovation?

When we think about the term - innovation, there are plentiful definitions. According to the New York City Economic Development Corporation Innovation Index and the U.S. Department of Commerce, innovation is "the design, invention, development, and/or implementation of new or altered products, services, processes, systems, organizational structures, or business models for the purpose of creating new value for customers and financial returns for the firm." What I really like about this definition is that innovation is really about "value-generation," nothing more...nothing less because a company's ultimate goal is to add positive value to the customer's experience. For example, Wal-Mart and Amazon are two companies that capitalize on this concept.

To grow the next generation of leaders, I propose that organizations do three things: (1) create a culture of innovative thinking, (2) establish a vision that incorporates innovation, and (3) value the people component of innovation. Although they are not all inclusive, they provide a baseline for companies to grow and develop future leaders.

Create a Culture of Innovative Thinking

In 1985, I was a young lieutenant stationed at Camp Red Cloud Korea. During one of our many deployments with the Republic of Korea (ROK) Army, I had an idea that I thought would improve operations. I observed some physical things with the AN/TSQ-93 van that I thought could be better. You are probably wondering what in the world, is a TSQ-93. Simply put, it is a mobile van platform that we used in the 1980's to conduct command and control military operations while deployed.

After returning from the deployment, I began researching the process. I later submitted the *new idea* to the Air Force. After a thorough review and evaluation by a team of experts, my recommendation was deemed to have..." intangible benefits of moderated/limited value." Although my idea was not implemented, I was pleased to receive a plaque for my efforts. As a young Lieutenant, I was elated that the Air Force leadership had created a culture that encouraged young potential leaders to engage in innovative thinking.

In his 2011 book, *Open Services Innovation: Rethinking Your Business to Grow and Compete in a New Era*, Henry Chesbrough writes, "...no company can grow and prosper without new ideas...the changing needs of customers, increasing competitive pressure, and the evolving abilities of suppliers necessitate continual creative thinking."

Leaders who foster this type of environment become magnets for *attracting* people who are inquisitive; who ask thought-provoking questions, and are not bound by the status quo. Having a background in both chemistry and information technology, I have always had an inquisitive imagination. How can we make things better is what drives innovative leaders to create a culture of innovative thinking.

In 2012, I read an article in Forbes magazine by Jeff Dyer and Hal Gregersen entitled, *"How Innovative Leaders Maintain Their Edge."* In the article, Dyer and Gregersen discusses their 3-P framework which focuses on the relationship between the company and its people, process, and policies (which makes up the 3-Ps). How well a company leverages this relationship will differentiate the innovation thought leaders from their peers.

Innovative leaders do not just do innovation themselves. They systemically replicate their own innovation skills throughout their companies. Their goal is to grow the next generation of innovative leaders.

Establish a Vision that Incorporates Innovation

Innovative leaders are visionaries. They establish a vision that incorporates innovation as a major part of the growth strategy for the organization. They are always exploring new ideas.

When I think of innovative leaders whose vision impacted the world, Steve Jobs tops my list. He was a genius at inspiring innovation. Because of his vision, Apple literally has a worldwide following. People cannot wait to see what the next BIG THING from Apple will be.

When I was assigned to the Oklahoma City Air Logistics Center, the commanding general made innovation a part of the strategic fabric of the organization. Innovation for him was not just a "buzz word," but he believed that it could make a difference. He was passionate about innovation and made it a major part of his *commander's intent*.

As a maintenance depot and the largest Air Logistics Center in the Air Force, this organization was primed for innovative measures. Each business unit was tasked to explore ways in which we could improve operational effectiveness and efficiencies. A cross-pollination of ideas began to flow throughout the organizations.

As the Director of Information Technology and the Chief Information Officer for the Center, I personally served on several innovation improvement teams and witnessed the benefits of allowing individuals to think outside the box. From improving processes, procedures, systems -- to designing new tools to help the maintenance technicians perform their duties, I witnessed the power of innovation. I was amazed at some of the ideas that began to come forth from the different teams. Yet, it all started with the commanding general making innovation a part of his vision for the organization.

Value the People Component of Innovation

Innovative leaders recognize that people are the nucleus of any successful organization. Without the people, the mission would not be accomplished. Successful innovative leaders understand the intellectual capital that people bring to their organization. They are not a commodity, but are core contributors to innovative solutions and ideas. When challenged to grow and develop as innovative thinkers, these individuals can provide the basis for future leadership within the organization.

Successful innovative leaders recognize their limitations and are eager to develop their team. They understand the *law of maximizing the whole.* By hiring the right team players, they can reduce the level of failure by increasing the level of success. When a leader recognizes his/her limitations, it is not a sign of weakness, but strength.

CHAPTER SUMMARY

Innovation is a major driver of economic growth and prosperity. Who knows where the next innovative leader will emerge. Therefore, successful innovation leaders create a culture of innovative thinking. They establish a vision that incorporates innovation as a major part of the company's growth strategy. Innovation leaders value people and strategic partnerships. They are not afraid to embrace new idea generation. They encourage their team to think outside the box. Finally, innovative leaders promote continuous professional growth and development.

ൟ

CHAPTER 10

Leveraging the Strength of Diversity and Inclusion

D uring a 1976 speech in Pittsburgh, Pennsylvania, former president Jimmy Carter said, "We have become not a melting pot but a beautiful mosaic. Different people, different beliefs, different yearnings, different hopes, and different dreams." What an amazing descriptor when it comes to describing diversity. According to the Census Bureau, the United States population is becoming more multicultural and diverse. Today, the workforce reflects a barrage of different ethnicities and cultures worldwide. With their wealth of knowledge, experience, and innovative thinking, many of these individuals have become the catalyst for growth and expansion in their respective organizations. Since many of these individuals are multilingual, they have become major contributors to their companies' ability to reach a broader market. In order to preserve this level of success, effective leaders must master the art of *maximizing the leadership potential* of its multinational workforce. In principle, this becomes the heart of diversity.

When many leaders think about diversity, the term *compliance* appears at the apex of their action list. Is my organization in compliance with various requirements stemming from Title VII of the Civil Rights Act of 1964 and other related directives? How effective are my diversity initiatives? What metrics do I have to substantiate them? These questions and others dominate the thinking of many leaders.

Because of the legislation, there has to be an adherence to the law. Having served on the Secretary Air Force Inspector General's Team at the Pentagon many years ago, I understand and value the importance of compliance. Our office conducted numerous short and long-term investigations involving compliance issues.

Yet, at the epicenter of diversity is the inherent need of individuals to have their voice heard and their talents and abilities recognized. Diversity is not just about compliance but inclusion. When it comes to leader development, everyone deserves a chance to grow and advance as a leader. Therefore, opportunities for leadership training, education, and mentorship should be distributed equally.

Today, we live in a society in which diversity and inclusion across the entire spectrum of the organization matters. In order for leaders to be effective in today's global marketplace, they must recognize and harness the skills and talents of individuals from across the organization not just a "select chosen few."

When it comes to diversity, the military is an example of an institution that continues to progress in the area of inclusion. Over the years, the military has made significant strides in expanding its diverse leadership pool. For example, there have been several minority generals and admirals to reach the highest military rank—four stars. In the early 1990's, I had the distinct privilege to serve on the Joint Chiefs of Staff in the Directorate of Intelligence at the Pentagon when General Colin Powell was the Chairman of the Joint Chiefs. He was the first African American to hold this position. As a young Captain, this was a rewarding experience and a major highlight of my military career. General Powell would later serve as the Secretary of State.

Throughout my military career, I had the opportunity to serve under several high-ranking generals who proved that race is no barrier to leadership. Air Force Lieutenant General Albert Edmonds, Lieutenant General Ronnie Hawkins, and Brigadier General Walt Jones represent a few of the best leaders that I had the honor to serve under their leadership, tutelage, and mentorship. Since retiring, Generals Edmonds and Jones have both invested in our economy as entrepreneurs with thriving multi-faceted businesses.

Today, the military continues its mission to create a military leadership institution that reflects society. For example, Army General Lloyd Austin is currently serving as Commander of the United States Central Command, which is a combatant or warfighting command. This command was responsible for command and control of operations in both Afghanistan and Iraq. General Austin is the first African American to hold this position. On the other hand, General Larry Spencer, who has had a distinguished career as a leader, is the current Vice Chief of Staff of the Air Force. To my knowledge, General Spencer is the first African American to serve in this position.

Without hesitation, the military has made great strides in developing leaders from a diverse background. Despite this success, the number of females earning the highest military rank only recently improved over the last several years. According to public records, only three female officers have achieved four-star rank. Retired Army General Elizabeth Dunwoody was the first female to receive four stars. Several years later, Air Force General Janet Wolfenbarger became the second female to earn four stars.

On July 1, 2014, the Navy made history by naming its first female four-star admiral. Michelle Howard, a 54-year old African American became the 38th vice chief of naval operations. She is the first woman and African American to hold this position. In honor of this event, the Secretary of the Navy said, "Her accomplishment is a direct example of a Navy that now, more than ever, reflects the nation it serves—a nation where success is not born of race, gender, or religion, but of skill and ability." What a powerful recognition. The Secretary of the Navy's comments encompasses the true essence of diversity and inclusion.

Despite the progress made in our military, as a nation as a whole, we must continue to make strides in diversity and inclusion until the core of any leadership promotion is based on one's skill and ability – nothing more or nothing less. Afterwards, we as Americans can proclaim that we are truly a nation were opportunity for success is a reality and not a myth.

CHAPTER SUMMARY

For years, diversity has been viewed as a compliance issue. Many leaders have worked diligently to ensure that the compliance aspect of the legislation was achieved in their organizations. Yet, in some instances, the people most impacted by the legislation were still under represented at some of the most senior levels in the organization. Innovation is a major driver of economic growth and prosperity. Who knows where the next innovative leader will emerge.

To create a diverse group of senior leaders, the development, mentorship, and training of these individuals must occur early in their career. Therefore, when it comes to leadership development, leaders must provide opportunity for growth across the organization regardless of any external factor. Devising a leader development strategy to explore the abilities and skills of individuals is essential to creating a culture of inclusiveness.

❧

CONCLUSION

A ccording to several GAO reports, over the next five to ten years about 50 percent of all government agency managers will be eligible for retirement. Filling this leadership gap may require organizations to invest in employee leadership developmental programs that will enable their staff to cultivate and develop their leadership potential. At times, the results may not be immediate, but the positive seeds that we plant in their lives will eventually sprout and produce a fantastic harvest. As documented in numerous studies, human capital investment is essential for any long-term organizational strategic growth. Although technology plays a major role in organizations, people remain the primary catalyst for organizational success.

In *Gifted to Lead: 4 Steps to Releasing Your Leadership Potential*, we explored various definitions of leadership. Although there is no one definitive definition, one common denominator is always present – the leader's ability to influence followers. If the leader is unable to influence his or her team to action, then what degree of leadership is occurring?

In *Gifted to Lead: 4 Steps to Releasing Your Leadership Potential*, we also discussed how the CORE Leadership Development Model can help emerging leaders grow and develop their leadership potential. By using this simple, 4-step process (**cause, opportunity, response, and evaluation**), individuals can identify and cultivate their leadership skills. However, sometimes it may take a positive mentor-mentee relationship to propel individuals to expand their leadership horizons. As the leader or manager, you have the power to encourage employees to establish personnel stretch goals that will enable them to progress in their leadership development.

In *Gifted to Lead: 4 Steps to Releasing Your Leadership Potential*, we also discussed strategies for building a diverse leadership team through innovation, diversity and inclusion. In order for leaders to be effective in today's global marketplace, they must recognize and harness the skills and talents of individuals across the organization.

When it comes to leader development, everyone deserves a chance to grow and advance as a leader. Therefore, opportunities for leadership training, education, and mentorship should be distributed equitably across the organization. Since we all have gifts and talents, you never know who may be that next history-making leader.

BIBLIOGRAPHY

Agnes, Michael. (2004). *Webster's New World College Dictionary Fourth Edition.* Cleveland: Wiley Publishing.

Association, A. M. (2013). *6 Key Skills That Will Make You Indispensable.* Retrieved from http://www.amanet.org/training/promotions/six-skills-for-managers-and-leaders.aspx

Black, B. (2006). *From the Hood to the Hill.* Nashville: Thomas Nelson .

Broughton, L., & Dyer, P. (2011). *Victory: 7 Entrepreneur Success Strategies for Veterans.* Newport Beach: Bandera Publishing.

Collins, J. (2001). *Good to Great.* New York: HarperCollins Publishers.

Creswell, J. (2005). *Educational Research: Planning, Conducting, and Evaluating, Quantitative and Qualitative Research (2nd ed.).* Upper Saddle River: Pearson Hall.

Development, A. S. (2012). *2012 State of the Industry.* Retrieved August 2013, from ASTD Publications: http://www.astd.org/Publications/Research-Reports/2012/2012-State-of-the-Industry

Finzel, H. (1994). *The Top Ten Mistakes Leaders Make.* Colorado Springs: Cook Communications Ministeries.

Fuhrman, J. (2004). *Leading Leaders to Leadership: 21 Secrets for Leveraging Your Way to Greater Success.* Possibility Press.

George, J. (2012). *A Leader After God's Own Heart.* Eugene: Harvest House Publishers.

Gillam, M. M. (2013, June 6). *Effective Leadership and Change.* Retrieved June 6, 2013, from Ezine Articles: http://EzineArticles.com/?expert=Mary_M_Gillam

Hesselbein, F. (2002). *Hesselbein on Leadership.* Josey Bass.

Jones, G., & George, J. (2008). *Contemporary Management.* Boston: McGraw-Hill.

Kouzes, J., & Posner, B. (1995). *The Leadership Challenge: How to Keep Getting Extraordinary Things Done in Organizations.* San Francisco: Jossey-Bass, Inc. Publishers.

Maxwell, J. (1993). *Developing The Leader Within You.* Nashville: Thomas Nelson Publishers.

Maxwell, J. (1998). *The 21 Irrefutable Laws of Leadership.* Nashville: Thomas Nelson Publishers.

Maxwell, J. (1999). *The 21 Indispensable Qualities of a Leader.* Nashville: Thomas Nelson Publishers.

Maxwell, J. C. (1993). *Developing the Leader Within You.* Nashville: Thomas Nelson, Inc. Publishers.

Meyer, P. J. (2002). *The 5 Pillars of Leadership: How to Bridge the Leadership Gap (2nd Edition).* Mechanicsburg: Executive Books.

Munroe, M. (2003). *The Principles and Power of Vision: Keys to Achieving Personal and Corporate Destiny.* New Kensington: Whitaker House.

Neuman, W. (2003). *Social Research Methods (5th ed.).* Upper Saddle River: Prentice Hall.

Nickels, W., McHugh, J., & McHugh, S. (1999). *Understanding Business, (5th ed.).* Boston: McGraw-Hill.

Office, U. G. (2013). *Critical Skills & Competency (Publication No. GAO-13-188).* Washington.

O'Neil, W. J. (2005). *Military & Political Leaders of Success.* New York: McGraw Hill.

Orcher, L. (2005). *Conducting Research.* Glendale: Pyrczak Publishing.

Pace, R. (1983). *Organizational Communication: Foundations for Human Resource Development.* Englewood Cliffs: Prentice Hall.

Robbins, S. (2005). *Essentials of Organizational Behavior, (8th ed.).* Upper Saddle River: Pearson Prentice Hall.

Stahl, J. (2007). *Lessons on Leadership: The 7 Fundamental Management Skills for Leaders at all Levels.* New York: Kaplan Publishing.

Studer, Q. (2008). *Results that Last.* Hoboken: John Wiley & Sons, Inc.

APPENDIX 1

Workbook Exercises

L eadership development is not an isolated mission relegated to a single department in the company. It must be a top-down driven focus area that involves the entire organization. Growing and developing leaders is a major investment in human capital productivity. Encouraging individuals to develop their leadership potential produces mutual benefit for both the company and the employee.

The purpose of this workbook is to help emerging leaders discover their God-given leadership potential by presenting a series of thought-provoking questions. The questions are designed to inspire individuals to (1) find a leadership cause that they are passionate about, (2) seek out an opportunity to act, (3) respond in the affirmative, and (4) evaluate and learn.

121

The workbook is divided into three parts, which align with the sections in the book. Part I is "The Leadership Dilemma". Part II is "Understanding the CORE Leadership Development Model." Part III is "Building a Diverse Leadership Team Through Innovation, Diversity, and Inclusion.

Part I: General Leadership Questions

Below are a series of general questions to stimulate the leadership discussion.

1. How would you define leadership?

2. What are some of the traits of a successful leader?

3. How many of these traits do you possess?

4. How important is it for you to develop your leadership potential?

5. Would you categorize yourself as a leader?

6. Have you had any leadership development training in the past?

Part II: Understanding the CORE Leadership Development Model

Write down five **"causes"** that you are passionate about.

Prioritize the above five causes in the order of importance to you. Assign a value of 1-5, with 1 being the highest.

Now, if you were given the **opportunity** to act from a leadership perspective regarding this cause, would you do it? For example, if you were asked to organize a walk/run event or simply pull together a team of volunteers to raise awareness for this particular cause, would you do it?

Based on the cause(s) that you identified in the previous question, write down five **"opportunities"** in which you can get involved from a leadership perspective.

1.

2.

3.

4.

5.

Of the above five items that you identified, prioritize them in the order of feasibility. Can you accomplish any of the above opportunities in the next 90 days? If so, prioritize them. Assign a value of 1-5, with 1 being the most feasible.

1.

2.

3.

4.

5.

After prioritizing your items, take a few minutes to think about your answer. Now that you have identified several opportunities, what are you willing to do about them? Be honest with yourself. For it is through honesty that you can truly identify those barriers that will prevent you from becoming the leader that you were designed to be.

Responses can be categorized as (1) positive, (2) negative, (3) indifferent, or (4) other. If you were given a recent opportunity to lead an event, how did you respond?

Are there any specific things that influenced your response? For example, did fear of failure play a role in your response or lack thereof to the leadership opportunity?

Part III: Building Your Leadership Team Through Innovation, Diversity & Inclusion

How can innovation, diversity, and inclusion expand the leadership pool in organizations?

Does your organization have initiatives that inspire leadership through innovation, diversity, and inclusion?

APPENDIX 2

Leadership Characteristics

Q7. What are the characteristics of an effective leader?

1. Ability to inspire those supervised to give their best efforts in support of the organization. Set a good example. Have the ability to teach, redirect, and enforce rules, discipline fairly when necessary.
2. Communications expert; thinks outside the box and projects outcomes; open to ideas but can defend decisions in simple, direct terms. Knows the strengths of the people around them. Shares credit and recognizes the value of others. Recognizes strengths and weaknesses of the team members, but has faith and generosity in their role.
3. Treats people with respect.
4. Good listener.
5. Listens to others; a decision-maker.
6. Honesty, confidence, fairness, leadership, support.
7. Intelligent, good listener, decisive, willing to compromise.
8. Ability to give people who work for you credit for their accomplishments.
9. Someone who can get others to work as a "team" and do what they are individually supposed to do for overall team results.

10. Good communication with co-workers; assists with task/policy and procedures.
11. "Servant" leadership is very important, as it entails actually acting while leading, in order to effectively show what the end goal should be.
12. Open-minded, able to see problems from multiple angles, motivating, positive, willing to accept responsibility.
13. Charismatic, approachable, empathetic knowledgeable, able to teach, consistent.
14. A good leader must lead by example; be a hard worker, supportive, set clear guidelines, ethical, strive for impartiality, understanding, excellent communicator, value logic and reason, be broadly educated, and finally, know when and how to discipline.
15. Good motivator, high emotional intelligence quotient (IQ), good empathy, professional.
16. Ability to listen; think critically when making decisions and solving problems; be decisive.
17. Leaders must know their audience/co-workers. Gear your presentation or guidance in accordance with the knowledge of the people you are leading (i.e. do not talk over their heads or below them. You will lose your effectiveness as a leader if you engage in this behavior).
18. Lead by example.
19. Humility is essential.
20. Knowledgeable, fair, well-qualified, well-organized, inspiring.
21. Clear decision-making, good analytics skills, and great people skills.
22. Strong and assertive, yet compassionate.
23. Decisiveness, empathy.

24. Confidence, assertiveness, conviction of belief system to motivate the process.
25. Team player and coach; water carrier if necessary.
26. Lead by example; confidence, knowledge, kindness, strength, motivating.
27. Knowledgeable, effective, empathetic, motivating, approachable, helpful, understanding, and flexible.
28. Listener, team player, celebrates diversity, welcomes diverse viewpoints, makes everyone feel welcome, and ensures everyone is heard.
29. Ability to maintain order and obtain respect. Able to relate to the needs of the people you oversee. Able to be objective, but also able to make final decisions and make them work.
30. Someone with a very strong sense of right and wrong with enough confidence to stand alone.
31. Be respectful, consistent, open-minded.
32. Integrity, honesty, and openness.
33. Good listener, effective communication techniques, critical thinking and problem solving skills. The ability to make tough decisions when the need arises. An effective leader should also know their limitations and weaknesses.
34. Listen more than they talk. Know how to find the answers to questions. Encourage new ideas.
35. Effective communicator, able to think quickly and make good decisions; respected, intelligent, able to learn, passionate.
36. Someone who can motivate others to produce their best and let them do so their way, without interference.

37. Integrity.
38. Ability to make decisions; ability to take charge.
39. Trustworthy, strong communicator, flexibility, compassionate, consistent.
40. Good communicator; excellent motivator; fair/impartial/consistent.
41. Dedication and drive. Without these characteristics, no one can lead.
42. Decisiveness, organized, articulate, focus on important details in order to make good decisions, ability to learn and listen to others that are more knowledgeable in areas where one is not.
43. Inspires people to do their best, challenges but encourages people.
44. Leading by example.
45. Knowledgeable.
46. Having people to actually follow them.
47. Able to lead.
48. Ability to get people to come together for some purpose.
49. Ability to motivate others to get the job done.
50. Confidence, logical reasoning, compassionate.
51. Organized, creative, trustworthy, innovative.
52. Relating well to people.
53. Listening, responding in a timely manner, ability to manage others, ability to delegate.
54. Ability to communicate, ability to delegate, ability to inspire, honesty, creativity, sense of humor.
55. Charisma.
56. Lead by example, treat everyone the same.
57. Confidence.
58. Listens, learns, acts.

59. Take charge, know what you are doing, good communication.
60. Excellent communicator, leads by example.
61. Listen to those you are supposed to lead because they will listen to you if they feel like they are being heard. Have set rules and be well organized.
62. Motivated and gets along well with others.
63. Serving attitude.
64. Good listener; empowers the employees; helps employees; realize their potential and leads by example.
65. Fairness, vision, charisma, conviction.
66. Leader characteristics consists of being a strong role model, positive and clear communicator, develops and can communicate their vision, strong ethical base, commitment to their team, company, and to the larger community.
67. Confidence, knowledge, kindness.
68. Truth-telling, planning, speaking convictions, even handedness.
69. Take command without belittling those you are leading.
70. Listener, coach, mentor.
71. Good listener.
72. Honesty, integrity, communication.
73. Emotional intelligence, ability to clearly communicate.
74. Positive, good listening skills, supportive, confidence, passion for the job, confidence in those you are leading, thick skin, provides what subordinates need and gets out of the way, knowledgeable, humble, self-aware, able

to take criticism and give critical feedback effectively, trustworthy.

75. Good example, decisive, fair, protects underlings from directors.
76. Leads by example, listener, focused, driven, passionate, compassionate.
77. Being a person that represents characteristics of integrity, honesty, and fairness in the ways of conducting themselves in front of their peers.
78. Good communication skills.
79. Personality, organization, and outgoing.
80. Know when to step in and know when to leave things alone.
81. Leads by example.
82. Fairness, willingness to work with others, assertiveness, and multi-tasking abilities.
83. Strong personality.
84. Confident, honesty, communication, positive attitude.
85. Decisive, knowledgeable and organized.
86. Praise, encourage, and recognize others.
87. Listening, visionary.
88. Positive, conservative, powerful, willful.
89. Vision, facilitation, delegation, decisiveness, adaptability, strength of character.
90. Respect for others.
91. Trusted, integrity, visionary, encouraging, enthusiastic, motivated.
92. Ability to lead effectively.
93. Know the structure in order to get tasks done. Have the ability to assign jobs based on people's strengths.
94. Provide strategic direction; collaborative approach, and have a positive attitude.

95. Organized and logical, needs to listen and observe, sort meaningful information from background noise, then make decisions, communicate effectively, and motivate the team.
96. Positive attitude.
97. Motivated, optimistic, dependable, charismatic, honest, investigative, and consistent.
98. One who listens; always have ideas or suggestions to situations; ability to lead.
99. Charisma.
100. The ability to listen, motivate, delegate, challenge, accept feedback, persist and develop skills in others.
101. Listening.
102. A good listener.
103. Confident, knowledgeable, decision maker, listener, develop direct reports, manage the team, address problems and other situations, discover and solve the root of problems.
104. Responsible, team player, good listener, effective communicator, organized.
105. Diversity, leads by example, good listener, keen observation skills.
106. Honest, Reliable, Christian, Above Reproach.
107. Constant learner, good listener, can make decisions.
108. Listens well prior to responding; provide consistent responses both verbal and physical, not erratic. Willing to learn/understand how things work before giving own criticism.
109. Creditability wisdom passion.
110. Motivates, sets example, inspires without words, through minimal interaction can

        identify and bring out strengths that employees do not know they have.

111. Fair, respectful, supportive, and decisive.
112. Leading others to their best performance.
113. Honesty, support, perseverance.
114. Integrity, confidence, intelligence, follow-through.
115. Service to those beneath.
116. Being able to effectively communicate with those who you are leading. Making sure you present yourself in a fashion that you would like others to follow, which would include a strong voice and confidence.
117. Personal responsibility, consideration, effective decision making and communication skills.
118. Vision, purpose and ability to articulate the same.
119. Communication, ethics, morals, understanding
120. Firm but fair.
121. Charisma, organization, interpersonal skills.
122. Trust, guidance, assertiveness.
123. Good communicator.
124. Respect those they are leading, open to ideas, good listening skills, and effective decision making.
125. Strong communication skills, empathy and guidance.
126. Personnel example. Ability to be flexible but maintain high standards of conduct and performance.
127. Charisma, personality
128. Lead by example, good communication skills, knows how to utilize the resources at hand.

129. Trustworthy
130. Persuasiveness, able to facilitate cooperation in a diverse group, vision, and the ability to inspire.
131. Integrity, honesty, confidence, communication skills, supportive, persuasion, respect.
132. Intelligence, kindness.
133. Trust, reliability, honesty, sharing alike of failure and success, rewards.
134. Positive, matter of fact, knowledgeable, honest.
135. Motivation, communication, leads by example, honesty, integrity, moral and ethical.
136. Willingness to lead by example; takes calculated risks; supporting and encouraging to those around them; willingness to share the praise and accept mistakes.
137. Honesty, compassion, honor, loyalty, intelligence, wisdom.
138. Good communicator.
139. Passion, charisma, integrity, excellent communication and organization skills.
140. Being a person that others would want to work for; outgoing, responsible, honest.
141. Empathetic, team-oriented, calm, unflappable under pressure, fair, effective, possessing integrity, ability to recognize talent.
142. Organized, decisiveness, good listener, excellent communication skills, knowledgeable.
143. Confidence, intelligence, appearance.
144. Empathetic, honest, respectful, open-minded.
145. Ability to get people to work together to do things they could/would not otherwise do. After building 12 award winning (successful) teams over 30 years of service, I remain ready

to tackle and leadership opportunity or challenge. Today's government agencies need to push "manager" out the door and fill those slots with leaders. You will be surprised how efficient government can be with the right folks in the right jobs.

146. Communicator, coach, motivator, team builder, strategist, and planner.

147. Possess knowledge, confidence, and ability to work under pressure.

148. Listening/communication; willingness to serve.

149. Likes people.

APPENDIX 3

Congruency between Leadership Potential and Promotion Opportunity

Q9. Does developing one's leadership potential influence future promotion opportunities? Please explain.

1. I don't know, but it sounds reasonable to assume so.
2. I have only hired people eager to learn. Yes, it does.
3. Yes.
4. Yes, being able to lead should help increase your opportunities.
5. Yes. Employers want people who are able to take charge of a group and run a project.
6. You can prove your worth and desire to grow.
7. Not sure.
8. Of course.
9. Yes. If one doesn't go forward in one's development, he/she will not advance on the job.
10. If someone is well versed in leading and dealing with others, they can often transfer these skills to other jobs.
11. Yes.
12. Yes.
13. Yes. If you are able to motivate those you are in charge of, you will add positively to your organization.

14. I suppose so. It might prepare one for additional responsibility.
15. Yes, definitely. My MBA was instrumental in my promotion at work.
16. Probably, if one is interested in being promoted.
17. I believe it does. A leader is someone who goes beyond what is required. If an employee does not want to go the extra mile, then he/she will not be an effective leader.
18. Yes.
19. Infinitely. The more leaders there are within a group, the faster it can move to action.
20. Yes. Someone with greater drive and initiative is bound to be promoted more quickly.
21. Yes. A trained leader can utilize their maximum potential.
22. Yes.
23. Yes; assuming the individual wishes to make advancements.
24. Yes. A company can see that an employee is striving for leadership and looking for greater challenges in the workplace.
25. Yes. I would hope so.
26. Yes. Many places seem to be lacking trained leaders and managers. I feel as if most places would welcome trained leaders with open arms. Without proper management and leadership, the workforce can significantly suffer.
27. Of course; unless politics or people who do not celebrate diversity in the work force are involved in the process.
28. Possibly; may give a person the initiative to pursue higher goals.

29. Yes. Every employer would like an employee who actively tries to improve the business and the bigger an asset you are, the more money you should make.
30. It should. People like to follow leaders.
31. It depends on the job.
32. If you encourage your employees and members to be the best that they can be, then you will have smarter and more loyal employees and members.
33. Yes. Each organization will benefit by having effective leaders at all levels.
34. Unsure.
35. Yes. One's promotion opportunities stem from one's success in the job and that success relies on those who work for that person.
36. Yes. All organizations need effective leaders.
37. Yes. If you can't lead or manage human resources, it will be difficult for you to get promoted.
38. I don't think it should be a program that guarantees a promotion. I think it should be a tool for identifying who should make strong leaders and giving them opportunity to grow their skills.
39. Yes. Ideally one should have the leadership traits and ability that would qualify them for at least one level above their current position.
40. Yes. If you are known to be a leader you will get more responsibilities. Those then turn in to promotions.
41. Yes, even if they are not leaders. It teaches skills that are effective in jobs at almost every level of skill.

42. Yes, but is all depends on the success of the development. Much of leadership is common sense and understanding how to delegate without being too authoritarian, and there is only so much training you can do.
43. Leadership is a skill that is easily marketable and can transition to any job position.
44. Leads to future promotion.
45. Yes, unless they just want to work alone. If that is the case, they will get no advancement.
46. Yes.
47. Yes. If one is concerned with future promotion.
48. Yes, effectively initiating positive changes through leadership.
49. Yes, usually. Promotions, especially over time are likely to lead to jobs that require managing others and other types of leadership opportunities.
50. Probably.
51. It could only be helpful if the promotion was for a leadership position.
52. Perhaps. Depends on the organization.
53. Absolutely. Leaders know how to motivate.
54. No.
55. Yes. To move up in the company, you need to be in charge of more people.
56. Yes. We need leaders everywhere. Companies need them to make decisions because 95% of the work force is followers.
57. Yes. Companies would hire those with leadership training over those who don't have leadership skills.
58. Yes, even in the field of teaching. Teachers can become principals.
59. Yes.

60. Yes.
61. Yes. They are hand-in-hand. Promotion generally implies forward motion up the ladder.
62. Probably.
63. Yes, being willing and able to lead can open opportunities that only exist with a progressive career ladder.
64. Yes. If one can learn to be an effective leader then promotional opportunities should develop. Every business or organization is looking for good leaders.
65. Yes. Leadership potential is apparent from the earliest assignments. People interested in getting promoted must show progression in application of these talents.
66. Perhaps. Promotions are often based on whether an employee can handle a task and oversee projects to be completed before the deadline.
67. Yes. I look for candidates who have taken the time to develop themselves as a leader and for technical qualifications.
68. All areas of business need quality leadership in order to move forward.
69. Yes. You need to have leadership skills to be recognized in an organization.
70. Yes. It provides opportunities to grow and learn in order to become better at current position, and to move upward or outward.
71. If you can convince someone that you have leadership skills, they will give you a chance to practice them.

72.   I use to think so. I have taken many courses on leadership and just can't seem to get over the hump into the executive level.
73.   Yes. A leaders I someone who takes imitative and will usually be promoted faster than someone who does not.
74.   Yes.
75.   Sometimes. Many times, upper management does not want new leadership to threaten their status quo.
76.   Yes, because you get to experience some leadership skills.
77.   Yes, because a good leader will naturally move up the ladder.
78.   Yes. It allows them to build their character strengths.
79.   Yes, by taking on more responsibilities, your employer will notice.
80.   Yes. The more knowledge one receives the better they can serve a company.
81.   One can use their experience to show what they can provide the company.
82.   Yes, not all those who are performers are leaders.
83.   Yes, because it gives people who don't have time or funds for college degrees to better themselves.
84.   Certainly. It promotes broad-scoped thinking, creativity, empathy and impact.
85.   Adds value to the individual.
86.   None.
87.   Yes. Can't move forward effectively unless you are skilled at leading & managing others.
88.   Yes.

89.   Sometimes. It might take a good worker and put them where they do not produce best for them or the organization.
90.   Yes, because the core tenets of leadership can lead to improved performance from individual contributors and managers.
91.   Depends on the organization. However, it should.
92.   Yes.
93.   Yes, if such development increases workplace productivity.
94.   Yes. With education and knowledge, one can instruct or teach others the ways of obtaining future opportunities.
95.   Yes, makes promotion more likely.
96.   If someone was given tools to become an effective leader, they might manage people better.
97.   I believe so.
98.   No. Corporations hire who they want and promote who they like. No one with skills in leadership are just hired anymore.
99.   Promotions almost always trend to leadership positions.
100.   Yes. Everyone should be able to spearhead a committee, take charge of a project, or work collaboratively with others to get a job done.
101.   Absolutely. Within management it is vital.
102.   No. Doing the best provides promotion opportunities.
103.   Yes. If someone is ever to lead or supervise someone else, they need to already possess the skills.

104. Yes, it should. It would help the organization by having an experienced employee lead the new employees.
105. Yes, characteristics of leadership translate to success in positions.
106. Seldom. Most middle managers are indifferent leaders, and immediately feel threatened by superior leadership skills in those they manage. Any culture that only uses top-down evaluations to make promotion decisions tends to promote mediocre leaders.
107. Of course.
108. Yes, as long as developing leadership potential is not coupled with politics.
109. Yes, it makes an individual more vital in more capacities.
110. Strong leaders are always the first to be promoted.
111. Yes.
112. I think so. I would say it can be an effective way to create opportunities for others who may need it. You can find some diamonds in the rough.
113. Of course! There are very few jobs where advancement does not come with opportunities to solve problems.
114. Yes.
115. Given the position, it sure can.
116. Poster boy for the company.
117. Depends on one's career field and desire to lead or manage others.
118. No. Some people have it and some just do not.
119. Depends on position.
120. Yes. Being a good leader makes someone an obvious choice for a promotion.

121. Progression in management requires the ability to lead.
122. Not necessarily. Some positions in a company do not require leadership qualities.
123. Probably.
124. Shows interest in leading the success of the company.
125. Yes. Leadership is valuable for directing an organization and has long term benefits.
126. In a large corporation such as ours, yes.
127. Promotion comes from demonstrated leadership.
128. Yes. You must develop yourself in order to progress. No one is perfect so continuing to develop any skill, especially leadership skills, makes you more marketable in the long run.
129. Promotions almost always track with people having great leadership skills who gravitate toward people management positions as their career track, and for technological promotion for non-management tracks.
130. Yes. The more you know in all areas the more you can advance.
131. Potentially. If the leadership potential is developed and recognized, it can lead to other job opportunities.
132. Yes. Quite often the Peter Principle applies. Leadership development programs should help influence/deter this (hopefully).
133. Yes.
134. Displaying leadership qualities will increase the likelihood that one will be selected for a leadership position.
135. Yes and no. Yes, because natural leaders see things that can improve an organization and

tries to do something about it. No because leaders above them may hinder them for selfish reasons.

136. I believe it does. Most promotion opportunities extend beyond individual contributor roles and involve managing or supervising others. Someone who is a good leader would be effective in these types of roles and would be seen as a good fit for promotion opportunities.

137. Depends on the specific job. Some honestly do not require leadership potential. However, any position in a managerial role should. If you wish to advance your career in any leadership role, then I believe it would weigh heavily on promotion opportunities.

138. Yes, certainly. Having leadership potential is one of the keys to future promotions. Managing people requires someone with the ability to lead. Without it, it is extremely difficult to move into positions of increasing responsibility.

139. Yes. Many promotions are to positions where some type of supervisions of others occurs.

140. Yes. Each promotion either puts you closer to a leadership position, or makes you the leader of more people. Most managers who fail do so because they don't know how to lead.

141. Yes. Having the tools to effectively market your self is invaluable. If you can't explain why you are the right person for the job, why should you be considered?

142. It absolutely should. If one has the aptitude and can deal with the human relations sacrifices that leaders sometimes must make,

then they owe it to themselves and their workplace to seek training and enhance their abilities to lead. That said, there are some who will never be able to lead and will always do poorly as a team manager.

143. Yes. A person needs to be able to manage their work and projects. In order to do this they need leadership skills.

144. In some businesses, it would.

145. Yes, actively seeking a sought-after skill set definitely provides opportunities for advancement.

146. Makes one more desirable to the company.

APPENDIX 4

Correlation Between Response and Leadership Opportunity

Q12. When assessing leadership potential, does a person's response to a leadership opportunity reveal information about that individual's desire to lead? Please explain.

1. Not necessarily, it would depend on the opportunity itself and what type of leader a person wants to be.
2. No.
3. Yes there are cut out for it.
4. No, they could just be afraid of leading.
5. Yes. People who turn it down do not want that kind of responsibility.
6. Absolutely. Hesitation can lead to overlooked
7. Yes. If a person eagerly volunteers to be a leader, I believe that person has good leadership potential. Too often individuals are forced into leadership positions simply because no one else will take the role.
8. Not really. A lot depends on the situation at the time.
9. Definitely, since confidence has a lot to do with leadership.
10. Willingness, drive.
11. Yes, if a person declines an opportunity but is already committed to a leadership role in a project in process that would show commitment to the original project. If a person is reluctant to lead it could show a

lack of initiative lack of sufficient knowledge of the project.

12. It may, but also may mean one merely aspires to a higher position.

13. It can, since I was unable to put in the time for that particular opportunity due to having a child. That doesn't necessarily mean I am not interested in being a leader.

14. It depends on the opportunity as it relates to the persons interests or abilities.

15. Yes, however, the individual must know what he is doing or again the
effectiveness of his leadership is down the drain.

16. Yes.

17. Yes, the fear of failure will result in the same.

18. Yes.

19. Not always, but most likely.

20. Yes.

21. Of course it does.

22. Yes, usually a person that thinks they have something to add will accept the responsibility and move forward.

23. Not necessarily. I have found people who want the title and authority, who have zero leadership skills.

24. Yes. If they don't really want to be a leader, then they probably wouldn't excel in a leadership role.

25. Possibly. Sometimes there are other reasons as to why a person would struggle leading or decline a leadership opportunity.

26. Yes.

27. Yes, people exhibit leadership qualities and desires when presented with the opportunities.

28. For the most part. An occasional denial of leadership would not be a problem, but with repeated refusal I would worry.

29. Yes. If the person passes on a leadership opportunity, he/she may not have a desire to lead.
30. A great leader doesn't take you where you want to go. They take you where you need to go.
31. Not necessarily. The reason for declining may valid.
32. No, just because an individual accepts or wants to lead an assignment does not make them a leader
33. Yes, because an effective leader does not necessarily need to know the subject area. That will come with the job eventually. Someone who doesn't want to be in a leadership role, especially after training, should not be in one.
34. Their response demonstrates their ability to evaluate an opportunity.
35. People who are too reserved or passive are seen as ineffective.
36. Yes. Their response will reveal what they are looking to achieve by taking a leadership role. The motivations will also likely impact their ability to lead effectively.
37. Often.
38. Yes, if a person is unsure about what should be done they are showing a lack of faith in themselves.
39. Not necessarily, some very humble people have become great leaders
40. This question makes no sense.
41. Yes. If they lack the desire to lead they might also lack the knowledge or training to lead.
42. Yes.
43. Not always. They may just not want to lead that particular project.
44. Probably. Situation determines response.
45. Yes, if you don't want to try then you don't really want to lead.

46. I would think it often does, of course that doesn't necessarily have anything to do with the individual's ability to lead.
47. Maybe.
48. I don't know.
49. No. Some of the greatest leaders initially had no desire to lead, while some of the poorest leaders only want to be in a position of authority, without having any idea how to exercise authority.
50. Usually. If a person does not take the opportunity to lead, it may indicate fear or lack of self- confidence.
51. No.
52. Yes, if the really want to lead, they will push for it.
53. Yes. Never accept "maybe". If he is a leader, he will welcome the challenge.
54. A good leader will find a way to get a project done.
55. Not always. Some people desire to lead but may feel unsure about leading for various reasons, especially if they have never led before.
56. No.
57. Yes.
58. No, it actually means they are wise and know when it is best to step forward.
59. It probably does most of the time. I can imagine scenarios in which this may not be the case but it seems a moot point: how else would one determine whether an individual desires leadership?
60. It may. In some cases a commitment to accepting the responsibility of leadership could be against an individual's best interests. That does not mean that they are uninterested or unable to lead.
61. Yes, if the person turns down opportunity then you question if they really have the confidence and skills to lead.

62. Yes, however, one must understand the reason(s) for declining the opportunity.

63. There might be temporary personal reasons, which should have little or no information about the person's desire to lead.

64. Not exactly-sometimes situations are outside the comfort zone or ethics of an individual.

65. Yes, it gives you a good sense of that person's self-awareness. some people are over confident in their abilities and do not realize they do not have the skills needed to take on those added responsibilities and others are too lacking in confidence to take it on.

66. Not always, each situation needs to be reviewed independently.

67. It demonstrated their feeling about their abilities as a leader.

68. Yes - it shows whether they have self-awareness or if they are self-important.

69. If you don't want to lead you will not be a stable leader and the position will soon be vacated again.

70. Yes. Leaders are usually willing to learn and adapt at every opportunity.

71. Not necessarily because the way one may choose to follow or lead in certain circumstances may just illustrate that the leader is wise to know how to function the best in different teams.

72. Yes.

73. Yes. Are they giving legitimate reasons for declining or merely coming up with an excuse?

74. No.

75. Yes if that person is unsure or unwilling then that person lacks confidence.

76. Yes, lack of interest equals lack of ability.

77. Yes.

78. Yes, willingness to take on a project in leadership capacity shows self-assurance.

79. No, the timing may not be right for the person.

80. No, as some leaders may not know that they have the qualifications to be a leader or don't know how to take that step to become a leader.

81. No.

82. Yes, to an extent. It may reflect reticence, but it also may reflect judgment about what kinds of leadership tasks one should accept vs. decline.

83. Yes, if you want to lead, you will.

84. None.

85. It can, depending on circumstances and reasons for the response. There are valid reasons for turning down leadership opportunities.

86. Yes.

87. No, it can mean they are content.

88. Yes, generally speaking, leaders seek to expand their roles and responsibilities and challenge them.

89. Sure - but be careful.

90. Yes, eager to lead indicates ambition and self-confidence.

91. Yes, most people have the inner desire to lead but are not recognized.

92. No.

93. Some people are in leadership positions for power. An effective leader may want power but their goals are to lead with humility.

94. No

95. No.

96. Yes. If a person does not take opportunities to lead there may not be a desire to be a leader. Or there may be fears associated with being the leader.

97. No, there are some very qualified leaders in my school but not all have the time to take a leadership

role or may not have the means to get the job done correctly.

98. Not in all cases some people just need the forward push to accept and even embrace leadership.

99. I do not understand the question.

100. It does but other factors should be taken into consideration like what other things the person is leading.

101. Yes, it may.

102. Yes motivation and interest relate to learning and desire.

103. Not necessarily. Too many factors can lead to an individual's decision to not seek or to decline an offered leadership position.

104. Yes, they may be afraid and will turn it down

105. No. The opportunity may be outside of the person's competencies.

106. Yes, eagerness, enthusiasm, initiative show greater leadership potential.

107. Depends on the reason they declined.

108. Yes.

109. I think it does. It's similar to applying for a job in that you always want to make a good impression; although I don't believe that the initial perception of someone based on body language in a moment or two should disqualify them from reaching their full potential.

110. Yes, sometimes. A refusal to lead can be a sign of preparation for leadership, depending on circumstances.

111. Yes, cooperation with leadership is important.

112 No, there are people that want to lead but by past experience are not able to get the project.

113. Yes.

114. I don't understand the question.

115. No. That situation may not be what the individual is looking for.

116. No. Someone who is good at leading might decline for a number of reasons not relating to their abilities.

117. Not necessarily there may be extenuating circumstances.

118. Yes. Those seeking to develop and improve their own leadership abilities show a desire to want to lead and are good leaders.

119. Yes.

120. A positive response to a leadership role is taking a lead.

121. Yes. A certain degree of drive is useful for leading.

122. Not necessarily. Some of the best leaders must be discovered and coached. Desiring leadership isn't the same thing as being a good leader.

123. No.

124. Yes. Their response is a direct assessment of their desire to lead.

125. Not necessarily - the decision to accept/deny leadership opportunity is based on a myriad of factors, not solely on the desire to lead. If someone turned down an opportunity, would need to understand why before assuming they don't have the desire.

126. No explanation is possible - too vague.

127. Yes, Typically if a person has a desire to do something, he or she will seize any opportunity to partake in the activity.

128. Some people are just waiting for the opportunity, others create their own opportunities, and a few just need to be put in a position where they find that out about themselves.

129. Sometime yes, other times it's inflated ego or a willingness to delegate but not lead.

130. Yes, declining a leadership opportunity might be taken as a lack of desire. It could also be based on other factors, such as a recognition that the particular opportunity was not one for which the person selected was qualified.

131. It can. Many individuals have this. It needs to be encouraged.

132. Definitely. Leaders are eager to take on leadership opportunities and if a person does not seem excited by the opportunity, they will most likely lack the passion (although not necessarily the skills) required to be an effective leader.

133. Of course it does. If the desire is not there they should not be offered the opportunity. There are also differences here. Some individuals do not know that they have the leadership qualities that a good leader can spot. If they were to be molded and shaped then the opportunity should be given to them.

134. Yes, but it depends on the circumstances. If someone turns down an opportunity to lead a project or team, it calls into question their confidence and skills. But this could be corrected with additional career development.

135. Yes.

136. Of course. If I decline an opportunity or do a half-hearted job, I don't desire a leadership position. However, this is something that needs to be evaluated on a regular basis - just because I wasn't ready for a position last year doesn't mean I don't feel I am ready now.

137. Not always, some people project themselves differently to hide their motive.

138. Yes, it does. If one tries to reason why they are not a good fit for the position or that they'd rather stay where they are, then they are probably RIGHT! Just stay... However, if they instead seek the leadership opportunity challenge, educate themselves on any knowledge / experience shortfalls, and make that job
their own, there's almost no way to fail! Positive attitudes are contagious, and our best leaders lead by example.

139. Not always. There are many factors that must be evaluated such as family responsibilities or other projects that may be underway. A good leader will acknowledge when they do not have the required time needed effectively lead or oversee a function or project.

140. Yes, it will show what traits the person possesses

141. Yes; if given the chance, most people who want to lead. They will jump at the offer.

142. Yes.

APPENDIX 5

Correlation of Passion with Cause

Q13. Some people believe that passion influences leadership. Can activating one's passion concerning a particular "cause," motivate an individual to step out of their comfort zone and assume a leadership role regarding that cause?

1. Yes, of course If a person is passionate about a cause, and that person believes his/her involvement will advance that cause, then he/she is likely to join.
2. Every successful non-profit company requires passion, or the mission is a waste of time. Raving fans of businesses come from perceived passion.
3. The desire has to be there.
4. Yes, passion could be infective.
5. People who have no great desire for leadership may be eager and effective leaders in areas they are passionate about. An example would be fundraising for a disease that has affected someone close to them.
6. Yes. Giving someone an opportunity to prove themselves in a situation that is more desirable or passionate for them, gives them confidence to take on more difficult situations.
7. Absolutely. Often times when a person is dedicated to a cause, they will take command to make sure certain actions occur.
8. I believe that people with leadership abilities will help organize and run anything that is offered them. If you don't know details, learn them.

9. Definitely. Passion can make people find time and resources that they would otherwise avoid.

10. In certain instances, based on what someone's passion is.

11. Yes, if it is a project you believe in or invested in, you are more willing to take risks.

12. Yes, passion can allow a person to overlook their natural reservation or lack of self-confidence and be an effective leader.

13. Yes, it may, if one believes strongly in a cause.

14. It can, but not in all cases. Some people just do not feel comfortable in leadership roles, no matter how passionate they are about a cause.

15. Yes. A person's passion for a cause can make a good leader, at least for a time.

16. In certain circumstances it will cause a person to get out of their comfort zone. Again he has to know the subject to do that.

17. Yes.

18. Absolutely. This is how one can lead by example because of their beliefs.

19. Yes.

20. Yes.

21. Yes.

22. Having a vested interest in a cause is very motivating.

23. Yes, I think a cause that one believes in will motivate one where in different circumstances one may decline the leadership role if they have no strong belief one way or the other.

24. Yes, I think as a leader you want your team to succeed. If you are passionate about your team or cause, you will go the extra mile.

25. Yes, I agree. If you're passionate about something - it won't feel like work and you will be able to

motivate others to work with you to achieve your goal!

26. Yes. If someone is passionate about something they are more likely to want that something to succeed therefore stepping up and leading to help that something succeed.

27. Nothing great is ever achieved without passion. If you believe in a cause passion is contagious.

28. Yes. If they feel strongly about a position they are more apt to lead it.

29. Yes, when a person truly cares about a cause, they are more likely to get other people involved in said cause.

30. If an individual becomes passionate enough to see the type of change they want to occur and then they decide to take action it does influence their decision.

31. It helps if leaders are on board with the project.

32. Yes, if people are impassioned they often will leave their comfort zone to do many things.

33. Passion for something and leadership are not the same thing. One may have passion but be so ineffective at leading that the cause it hurt. However, the smaller the job, the less effective a leader has to be.

34. Their passion & knowledge will enhance their leadership.

35. This question appears incomplete so I don't know how to answer it.

36. Yes, passion can motivate. However this can also blind a leader to other associated issues, miss the big picture, or ignite irrational emotional responses to opinions contrary to the cause.

37. Yes, but some individuals just naturally assume command / leadership of a group.

38. Yes, it has been seen many times due to a recent court case in which people that have no training have "led" groups in protests.

39. Depends on the person. Everyone's motivation factors vary.

40. Yes. Again, this question is confusing because obviously you expect yes to be the answer. What do you really want to ask?

41. Yes. If people are passionate about a certain area than it would cause them to go outside their comfort zones more.

42. Yes, it can.

43. Passion can sometimes influence leadership abilities, but only to the extent of their knowledge.

44. Passion is vastly overrated. Concept of duty is what is important.

45. Yes.

46. Certainly, if one is very passionate about something, he/she may be able to get over any hesitations he/she would have to assume the leadership role.

47. Perhaps.

48. Yes, I have experienced this first hand, when I have taken leadership of a group because no one else was willing to, and it was my passion for this thing that made me realized that I had to do something to encourage its growth.

49. Yes. Being passionate about something can diminish or eliminate self-consciousness or self-doubt.

50. Yes. If someone is normally reluctant to lead but has a burning desire for a particular "cause" they step forward.

51. No.

52. Yes, passion will push you past you boundaries.

53. There are numerous things that influence accepting leadership. Passion is only one of the many.
54. Yes, of course. Motivation is what gets something done.
55. Yes!
56. Yes.
57. Yes.
58. Yes, but it can also be deceiving as once the passion goes away, so does the interest.
59. Maybe, but this may not be a good thing.
60. Yes, passion can be a powerful tool for a leader. And yes, I have seen people who I would not characterize as leaders transform into strong leaders when they have been faced with a cause they suddenly relate to.
61. Yes, I believe if a person is passionate for a cause they can put their insecurities on the back burner and step into a leadership position.
62. Sure, these are especially valuable opportunities to assess leadership potential. Is the person willing to learn before, during and after the opportunity? Is he/she willing to make mistakes, take risks, assess results, evaluate contributions, etc?
63. Yes, many people's passions lead them to conduct themselves in specific ways.
64. I don't believe that passion, in and of itself, can solely motivate a person to step out of their comfort zone. I think that in addition to being passionate the person must also feel comfortable in the role and have confidence.
65. Yes, but too much passion can skew their view and have adverse effects.
66. Yes but need to communicate the passion effectively.

67. Yes - the more connected the leader, the more effective - and the more invested s/he is with their opportunity.

68. Yes, because it motivates them sufficiently to inspire the kind of constant attention required in management.

69. Yes. If someone believes in or enjoys the cause more effort will be put forth.

70. I think the passion is either there or it is not. I don't feel that the passion for something can just be turned on like a switch but it is something that is shaped from the experiences of someone's life. Example, if someone was affected by a lost loved one in a cancer battle, that person may have a passion for cancer prevention and awareness.

71. I think so.

72. Absolutely! Most people will do a lot more if they believe in the cause. That's why it's important to get people "invested" before handing them a project.

73. Yes, I do think passion can influence leadership potential.

74. Yes, passion will give the courage that the person would otherwise lack.

75. Yes, it does.

76. Yes, if you're passionate about and idea and nothing is being done, people will take control.

77. Yes, the more a person believes in a process the more they are willing to step up and work hard.

78. Other people can see enthusiasm, which can lead to others wanting to follow a leader.

79. I don't think all those who have a passion are leaders.

80. Yes this is possible.

81. Passion is essential to great leadership...informed passion, not blind passion or ideology or self-

righteousness. Watch out for the difference between ego-driven' needing' to lead and having a passion for a cause that makes one a natural choice to lead.

82. Passion is a stimulant.

83. No.

84. Yes. One's passion can ignite a desire to step out of your comfort zone in order to accomplish a perceived "greater good".

85. Yes, it does.

86. Yes, because you must do what is best for yourself even if means pushing your limits.

87. Agree.

88. Absolutely. But passion alone leads to many crappy leaders - - - think of the children's crusade.

89. Yes.

90. Definitely, existing knowledge and personal knowledge about any area is great motivation.

91. Yes, I do believe that passion has some influence on motivating people.

92. Yes.

93. Absolutely. Taking the ownership for moving a cause forward is something that people do every day. How well they lead is another thing. Some people have ideas and others have the ability to make it happen.

94. No, there are many factors to a leadership decision.

95. Yes, motivated people can do just about anything they desire. If you want a leadership position motivation would have to play a part.

96. Absolutely. It is easier to lead in a situation in which a person is passionate about because that is the big motivator and there is a much stronger desire to do well and have those you lead to do well.

97. Someone comfortable in an area where they may have expertise may not lead them to take charge.

98. Yes, however it does depend on how the influence affects some people in good and bad ways

99. Yes. Passion causes people to be motivated.

100. Definitely if someone cares about and has bought into a cause they are more likely going to make space to lead

101. Not necessarily. A person may have passed that time in their life.

102. Yes, especially if passion is stronger than the comfort zone.

103. Yes, but the cases would be limited in the type of example given. If only a very specific cause motivates an individual to step beyond their comfort zone and assume a leadership role, that's passion, not leadership, per se. However, passion does influence leadership insofar as those leaders who show passion themselves and inspire it in others often are very effective leaders.

104. Yes, if you are passionate about something, it's not just a job for you, it is a belief system.

105. No. A person's charisma is not the inspiration for motivation.

106. Yes, there is a motivator with purpose that cannot be replicated extrinsically.

107. Sure! Passion is a strong motivator!

108. Yes.

109. Absolutely. If someone is passionate about something for a good cause (running a successful business, for example) I think it can unlock a person's passion to do more. And I think with that passion behind the cause, it's all the better.

110. Yes. Leadership frequently falls back on the will of the leader. Will is enhanced by passion.

111. Yes; interest is essential to lead effectively.

112. Yes, I think this statement is correct.

113. Very true.

114. Yes.

115. Unsure.

116. Yes. Being an introvert, I know that if I am passionate enough about something I will want to be involved even if it makes me a bit uncomfortable.

117. Passion can be a driving force for change including finding leaders where there was no plan prior to it. The passion can be too strong to ignore.

118. Although passion will make a person work beyond the "comfort zone", it does not necessarily equate to good leadership. Passion will often times limit a persons

abilities to being a good leader because judgment is made emotionally instead of rationally.

119. Yes, if they have passion/care then they will be more likely to work at that role.

120. Commitment to the goal shows a willingness to see a project or program to fulfillment which may include taking a leadership role.

121. I believe so. Purpose in life drives bold choices.

122. My leadership has been all about passion. That's where my teams have been the most successful.

123. Yes.

124. A passionate response indicates a desire to lead.

125. Of course!! If you're passionate about something, you'll be excited and your excitement on the subject naturally draws people in.

126. If your passion is great enough perhaps, this would help counteract discomfort.

127. Yes If an individual has a personal goal or cause they often are more comfortable or confident in leading others concerning the subject.

128. Yes, passion does influence leadership. Passion reflects motivation and desire to accomplish something and you cannot be an effective leader unless you want to accomplish something.

129. In some cases yes, particularly when a cause is personal to someone.

130. Yes, if one is passionate one is more likely to take the initiative in moving a "cause" or project forward.

131. Passion can provide the energy needed initially needed to lead.

132. I absolutely believe that passion influences leadership. Passion is what makes a leader someone that others want to follow, seeing them so very passionate about the particular cause inspires and motivates. Even introverts like myself jump up to lead in situations that we are passionate about.

133. Sure.

134 Yes - but passion by itself is not enough. A leader needs to possess real leadership skills and abilities, as well as passion, to be a successful leader.

135. Yes...if one has the passion, they take the reins.

136. Yes. Passion about a cause means you are willing to do what you can to help the cause. If you are brave enough, this can mean taking on a leadership role.

137. Passion can definitely motivate someone to step outside of their comfort zone if they are doing something that they care about.

138. Passion gets people motivated for good reasons, but does NOT always make them a good fit as a leader. Their own ideas may become more important than those of their task team, and they will eventually lose

team buy-in. The mission will fail, unless they can do it all by themselves.

139. Possibly.

140. Yes, I know from personal experience that I would step up in more of a leadership role on something that I am super passionate about rather than something I do not know much about.

141. Yes, I work with the homeless, and have assumed a leadership position in my organization because I was able to overcome my fears to better serve the people I work with.

142. People do lots for passion.

Speaker's One Sheet

STORY IDEAS

- How to Be a Top-Notch Leader Without Alienating, Bullying, or Destroying Your Team
- Triumph Against the Odds: If I Can Make It So Can You
- 4 Steps to Unleashing Your Leadership Potential
- What's Holding You Back? Is Fear Jeopardizing Your Career?
- How to Boost Your Leadership Potential and Accelerate Your Career
- What Makes Innovation Leaders Different? 7 Habits of Innovative Leaders
- How to Discover the Leader Within You
- 5 Things About Leadership that Every Leader Should Know
- No Excuses: You Can Lead, So Let's Go!
- Attention Ladies: How to Be a Dynamic Leader Without Becoming One of the Boys

Media Experience: Radio/TV/Digital & Hard Print

For speaking requests and more information about Dr. Gillam, visit her website at www.m2gleadershipbiz.com or email the author at gillammm@verizon.net

Keynote Speech Testimonial

Outstanding Speaker

"From the first phone call to the day of the event, Dr. Gillam was the consummate professional. She listened to our event theme and modified her talk to suit the people who would be in the room, most of which were small businesses. We were looking for a dynamic speaker to close our conference on a positive note; to encourage our local government contractors to look beyond the bounds of their current business model and customer base with the idea of expanding their horizons. In response, Dr. Gillam spoke on innovation. Her topic was,

"7 Strategies that Makes an Innovation Leader Different."

Her message was uplifting and encouraging, challenging our attendees to continue to grow and change, never letting their business practices becomes stale or stagnant. We were impressed with the way she presented herself and her message.

Deborah L. Jones, President & CEO, Prince William County Chamber of Commerce

Leadership Recognition Award

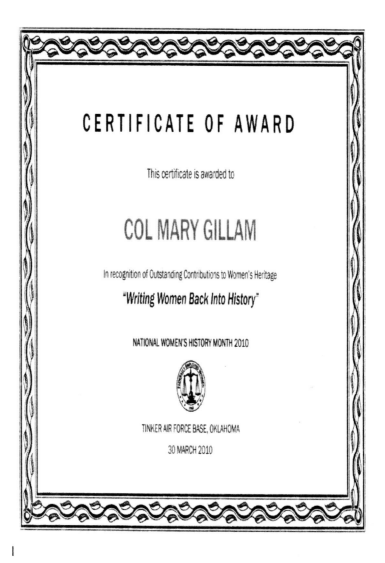

Thank You Note

Col. Gilliam, It has been a pleasure working for you. You have been the embodiment of great leadership and class and you shall truly be missed. I couldn't put in words how great a leader that you are so I found this poem to describe what type of leader I believe you are to me.

When leaders make a mistake,
they say, "I was wrong."
When followers make mistakes,
they say, "It wasn't my fault."
A leader works harder than a follower
and has more time;
a follower is always "too busy"
to do what is necessary.
A leader goes through a problem;
a follower goes around it and never gets past it.
A leader makes and keeps commitments;
a follower makes and forgets promises.
A leader says, "I'm good, but not as good as I ought to be;"
a follower says, "I'm not as bad as a lot of other people."
Leaders listen;
followers just wait until it's their turn to talk.
Leaders respect those who are superior to them and tries to learn
something from them;
followers resent those who are superior to them and try to find chinks in their
armor.
Leaders feel responsible for more than their job;
followers say, "I only work here."
A leader says, "There ought to be a better way to do this;"
followers say, "That's the way it's always been done here."

~ Author Unknown ~~

I wish you well!
Keith Hardiman

Congratulatory Note from
Lt Gen James Clapper

DIRECTOR DEFENSE INTELLIGENCE AGENCY

24 November 1992

THRU: Director, Office for Current Intelligence,
Joint Staff and Command Support, J2

TO: Captain Mary M. Gillam, USAF
NMIST Branch
Crisis Response and Exercise Division
Office for Operational Readiness
Directorate for Current Intelligence, Joint
Staff and Command Support, J2

It's my pleasure to join Admiral Jerry O. Tuttle, U.S.
Navy, Director, Space and Electronic Warfare, Navy
Department (N6) in expressing appreciation for the
excellent support you provided during the conference
between CNO, CINCLANTFLT, and USS GEORGE WASHINGTON.

Your administrative support, dedicated team work, and
attention to detail contributed significantly to the
overall success of the conference. Once again, I'd like
to thank you for your continued support.

1 Enclosure a/s   JAMES R. CLAPPER, JR.
Lieutenant General, USAF

cc:
J2R
J2R-1
J2R-1C

Congratulatory Note for Selection to the SCOPE EAGLE's List (Leadership Program)

3 February 1995

HQ ACC/SC
180 Benedict Ave, Suite 209
Langley AFB VA 23665-1993

Major Mary M. Gillam
55 CBCS/CC
575 10th Street
Robins AFB GA 31098-2236

Dear Major Gillam,

It's my great pleasure to congratulate you on your selection to the Scope Leader list by Air Combat Command. The selection this year was done through a panel review and only the strongest survived. While selection to the list does not guarantee a Scope Leader position, it is a strong indicator of the potential you have and we expect the best from you!

Your selection indicates that you are among the top performers within the ACC Communications-Computer and Audio Visual career areas. We're proud to have you as a member of the hard working, hard playing, ACC team and we look forward to continued success. Again, congratulations and best wishes in your continued Air Force career.

Sincerely,

JOHN L. WOODWARD, JR. Brig Gen, USAF
Director
Communications-Computer Systems

Air Force Cadet Officer Mentoring Program Recognition

AFCOMAP, Inc.
P.O. Box 47015
Washington, D.C. 20050

3 MAY 1999

Lieutenant General Nicholas B. Kehoe
Secretary Air Force Inspector General
1140 Air Force Pentagon
Washington, DC 20330-1140

Dear Lieutenant General Kehoe

    On behalf of the Air Force Cadet Officer Mentor Action Program (AFCOMAP), it is my genuine pleasure to express sincere appreciation to Lt Col Mary M. Gillam for her extraordinary leadership as the Co-Chair of the Pentagon sub-committee for the AFCOMAP 10th Anniversary Banquet Committee. This commemorative banquet was held on March 6, 1999, at the Capitol Ballroom, Bolling AFB Officer's Club. The banquet was a total success! You could see from the look of interest and excitement on the faces of the attendees, ranging from Junior Reserve Officer Training Corps (ROTC) and Air Force ROTC cadets to general officers - the message of mentoring hit home!

    AFCOMAP is an Air Force-sanctioned, non-profit organization committed to promoting professional leadership development of Air Force officers and assisting new officers with their transition into the active duty Air Force. The theme for the anniversary banquet was "AFCOMAP Mentoring for the New Millennium."

    Lt Col Gillam's superb leadership, superior communicative skills and her ability to motivate others contributed to the tremendous success of this commemorative banquet! Please present the attached certificate of commendation to her for a job well done!

    Sincerely

CLAUDE M BOLTON JR., Maj Gen, USAF
AFCOMAP Pentagon Senior Advisor

Attachment
Certificate

"Strengthening Future AF Leaders Through Mentorship"

ABOUT THE AUTHOR

Dr. Mary M. Gillam, President and CEO of M2G Dynamic Leadership Solutions, LLC, is a #1 Amazon best-selling author of over nine books. A retired Air Force Colonel and former member of the Senior Executive Service (SES) Corps with the Department of Defense, Dr. Gillam is an internationally recognized motivational speaker, coach, consultant, and trainer. She has been featured in numerous television, radio, and print media worldwide.

After military retirement, Dr. Gillam worked as a government contractor for Booz Allen Hamilton where she supported the Secretary of the Air Force Chief Information Officer (CIO) at the Pentagon. She was later appointed to the SES Corps, where she served as the Director of Technology, Innovation, and Engineering in the Office of the Secretary of Defense. Destined to fulfill her God-given purpose, Dr. Gillam took a leap of faith, and decided to start her own information technology and leadership development, consulting firm. Dr. Gillam is the creator and developer of the CORE Leadership Development Model.

A North Carolina native, Dr. Gillam was raised under very humbling conditions by her paternal grandmother. Because of her grandmother's love, faith, and tenacity, Dr. Gillam honored her memory with a special book in 2010. The book was entitled, *I Never Said Good-bye."*

Having spent over 30+ years working in telecommunications and information systems technology, Dr. Gillam is a strong advocate for the science, technology, engineering, and math (STEM) disciplines. She is a former chapter president of the Armed Forces Communications-Electronics Association (AFCEA), where she established a STEM related professional scholarship. She has held numerous leadership, management, and technical positions in her profession.

Dr. Gillam holds a Bachelor of Science degree in Chemistry, a Master's degree in Computers & Information Resources, a Master's degree in National Security & Strategic Studies, and a Master's degree in Management. She also earned a Doctorate degree in Management Information Systems Technology, a Graduate Certificate in Applied Project Management, and a Graduate Certificate in Legislative Studies.

A certified John C. Maxwell Leadership Speaker, Coach, and Trainer, and an experienced and seasoned leader, Dr. Gillam has won multiple military and civic leadership awards

For speaking requests and more information about Dr. Gillam, visit her website at www.m2gleadershipbiz.com or email the author at gillammm@verizon.net

❧

"Are you a *SERVANT* Leader or just a leader waiting to be served?"

—Dr. Mary M. Gillam